TWO SCREENPLAYS
(in Correct Spec Format)

A Window in Time

A Summer
with Hemingway's Twin

Screenplays and Introductions
by Dave Trottier

First Applewood Arts Edition
10 9 8 7 6 5 4 3

ISBN: 978-1-885655-15-0

Applewood Arts
4456 Manchester St.
Cedar Hills, UT 84062

Cover design by Daria Lacy

Dedicated to my clients and students
and to developing screenwriters everywhere

For a free subscription to my ViewsLetter, information about script consulting, free articles, and other cool screenwriting stuff, visit:

WWW.KEEPWRITING.COM
Email: dave@keepwriting.com
Facebook: facebook.com/keepdave
Twitter: twitter.com/DRTrottier

Other books by Dave Trottier
The Screenwriter's Bible
Dr. Format Tells All
Double Your Creativity in 3 Hours
The Secret of Question Mark Cave (script)
How I Became Perfect

CONTENTS

A WINDOW IN TIME

by Dave Trottier

HISTORY & CONTENT

In 1997, I optioned *A Window in Time* to Hill Fields Entertainment for an ABC movie-of-the-week starring Scott Bakula. During pre-production, ABC backed out because a then-current weekly time-travel show dropped in ratings. Suddenly, time travel was "high risk." Thus, when the option period ended, the rights reverted back to me.

I let the script sit, but re-printed the first nine pages along with commentary in my book, *The Screenwriter's Bible.*

A few years ago, I dusted off the script and updated it (that is, replaced phone booths with smart phones, microfilm library searches with Internet searches, and even added a Smart Car). While engaged in updating, I realized that in my original script written in 1997, I had "invented" prototypes for the iPad and personal drone. Therefore, in this new update, I decided to call the "miniature computer" a "custom iPad mini" because that's essentially what it was. The drone is still called the "miniature helicopter" in the script; I didn't change the name of that.

I also reluctantly de-emphasized symbolic elements that were somewhat similar to *National Treasure* and *The Da Vinci Code,* even though my script preceded those works by several years. I was in love with those elements, but felt I had to "kill off those darlings" for this update. One thing I didn't change was the prediction that the Chicago Cubs would win the World Series in the future.

The original 1997 screenplay quickly attracted attention. Many who passed on the script said they "couldn't put it down" and that they were "deeply moved" at the end, but they were worried that it wasn't "hip" enough (the scouting references) and it wasn't "edgy." Interestingly, *Window* contains more violence than any of my other screenplays, and the "love scene" is as hot as I've dared to go, given my penchant for writing family friendly material. Ironically, the ABC teleplay version in seven acts that I created in the pre-production stage had even less of an "edge" than the original PG-13 screenplay you will read.

Certainly, the script has weaknesses, and I'll let you decide what those are. In terms of the writing, my initial goal was a "fast-paced action flick" that would (hopefully) contain no time travel paradoxes or holes. However, the characters wanted their story to be romantic as well as exciting, so I tried to do right by them, too. Thus, my stated genre is *high-stakes actioner and gripping romance*. I guess that makes it a date movie.

The primary image of this screenplay is a window. There are 57 references to windows in action and dialogue. In fact, the first image is an Egyptian temple window through which the light of the sun shines through. This story is about a window in time that admits passage to the light of the future, the light of self-knowledge, and the light of love.

How did I get the idea? I had a dream. *I was driving down the street. A car followed me and pulled up next to me. I looked at the driver and he was me!* That evolved into the scene on page 12 of the script. The script went through major changes during the writing process. For example, Skippy Grimm the petroleum geologist became Jake Dekker the NASA aeronautical engineer.

WHY PUBLISH THE SCRIPT?

There are many reasons for publishing this screenplay, but the following two stand out as the ones that motivated me to go ahead.

1. Clients and students have asked repeatedly to see a successful ***spec*** script that is written in correct format. That's because most scripts available to read are ***shooting*** scripts, but developing writers break in with a spec script which is usually more readable, more entertaining, and unencumbered with technical directions. Incidentally, I define "successful script" as one that has been sold, optioned, or produced.

2. I've received hundreds of requests from screenwriters that have read the first nine pages of the script in *The Screenwriter's Bible* for the remainder. They want to know: *what happens next?*

As you can see, I am publishing both of these screenplays mainly for instructive purposes. Why don't I publish one of my produced screenplays? There are too many legal hurdles.

ABOUT THE FORMAT

The script is in correct, industry standard, spec screenplay format. I may have broken or bent a couple of formatting conventions, and there are probably a couple of little things I didn't catch. The script appears in 10-point Courier New (rather than the standard 12-point) to fit the dimensions of this book, but it looks just right. The tabs are correct.

On occasion, I used the scene heading extension CONTINUOUS when I thought it was necessary for clarity. CONTINOUS means the indicated scene follows the previous scene continuously without any jump in time. In most such situations, the extension CONTINUOUS was not used because it was already obvious that the scenes were flowing continuously. The extension SAME means "at the same time" as the previous scene.

On rare occasion, I underscored a sentence or phrase of narrative description (action) and words of dialogue for emphasis.

The script is sufficiently lean. Only two paragraphs of narrative description are longer than three lines, and the speeches are generally short.

Only important sounds were placed in all-CAPS, and I included transitions (editing directions) in a couple of places where I had a dramatic reason to do so. There are no camera directions.

I hope you find the script both readable and enjoyable. If you have a question or comment about the writing or format, please contact me at dave@keepwriting.com.

A WINDOW IN TIME

by Dave Trottier

Dave Trottier
4456 Manchester St.
Cedar Hills, UT 84062
801-492-7898
dave@keepwriting.com

FADE IN:

A window of an ancient Egyptian temple frames the morning sun.

SUPER: "NEAR LUXOR, EGYPT"

It's an archeological dig. At the temple base, a man-sized hole has been blasted through.

INT. EGYPTIAN TEMPLE - SAME

Torches illuminate the figures of a dozen motionless workers, all wearing black headdresses obscuring their faces and heads.

They stand back against the single, circular wall.

At the center sits a four-foot tall marble pyramid, protected by Egyptian statues. One is of Thoth, god of magic and time.

A goateed SHEIK carefully touches the hieroglyphics on the wall, then gestures to the marble pyramid.

Quickly, several workers pry the heavy marble pyramid from its foundation and push it over. It CRASHES to one side. Silence.

There, at the center spot, stands the Eye of Ra -- a dark, metallic pyramid only six inches tall.

On each side of the pyramid's top section, a purple crystal glows.

The Sheik's eyes water -- awestruck. The workers are stunned.

The Sheik carefully picks the pyramid up -- almost expecting a jolt -- and examines it with wonder.

A THIEF disguised as a worker, strides up to the Sheik.

A knife flicks into the Thief's hand from under the sleeve, and quickly slashes the Sheik's throat.

The other hand snatches the Eye of Ra.

A WORKER attacks the Thief, but is repelled by a swift kick to the face. A flash of the knife severs ANOTHER WORKER's windpipe.

The Thief dashes through an opening covered by a canvas flap.

BLACKNESS

A foot KICKS open two window shutters.

INT. JAKE'S HOUSE - UPPER ROOM - DAY

Bold beams of sunlight burst through the large window.

JAKE DEKKER, 29, wearing an honest face and a NASA ballcap, and his best buddy MARK, are bathed in a shaft of white sunlight.

Mark gazes out the second-story window into the backyard lawn and beyond to a grove of orange trees, then up to a blue sky.

MARK
Beats the hell outa your condo.

The room's walls are covered with posters of military flying craft of all kinds. Miniatures hang by string from the ceiling. On a desk is a custom iPad mini near a computer.

JAKE
And no one knows about it. Got a generator downstairs. No mail-man, no sales-man, no meter-man...

MARK
... And no wo-man.

JAKE
I value my privacy.

MARK
If you saw the babe I met yesterday, you'd go public.
(slugs him in the arm)
I'll set ya up.

Jake crosses the room and twists the knob of an arching desk lamp. It hovers over a large drafting table like a flying saucer. Large metal blueprint tubes lie beside the desk.

JAKE
My one true love. And <u>you're</u> going to help me sell her.

His one true love is on the drafting table: the design of a black and angular helicopter. Mark sighs in amazement as he turns page after page of blueprint designs.

JAKE (CONT'D)
Outside will be kevlar, carbon fiber, and --

MARK
-- Didn't you just present something like this to top brass?
(sheepishly)
I heard... a rumor goin' round.

A loud WHACK from behind scares Mark. Jake grins. The wind has blown the shutter against the wall.

While Mark re-opens the shutter, Jake covertly grabs a small hand remote. It has a short antenna, control knob, and tiny TV monitor on its face. He pushes a button and moves the knob.

A miniature helicopter darts up to Mark's face like a humming-bird, and hovers. He jumps back in fright, waving his hands.

MARK (CONT'D)
Hell, Jake....

Jake looks like a teenager operating his remote. This is fun.

JAKE
Don't move!

Mark freezes and looks a bit scared as the silent mini-copter silently orbits his head. His eyes try to follow.

JAKE (CONT'D)
A new concept, Mark. Small, quick. Can slip anywhere. For rescue.

Jake lands the thing on Mark's head. Before Mark can grab it, it darts away.

Jake WHOOPS it up; he's having a ball. He then frowns as he answers Mark's question.

JAKE (CONT'D)
Yeah, NASA, the military -- they rejected it. Don't think it's do-able. Besides, they want the big gunships. Fire power.

MARK
(pointing at helicopter)
Hell, Jake, that's the centerpiece of your sales promo right there.

Jake signals Mark over. Mark gazes into the tiny TV monitor. As the helicopter flits about, Mark views different parts of the room in the tiny monitor. Jake chuckles, his face aglow.

MARK (CONT'D)
A TV camera. Boy, could I get an eyeful at the beach.

Mark almost pants. Jake manipulates the knob and the tiny chopper silently scoots away and bolts out the window.

EXT. JAKE'S HOUSE

The tiny chopper flies over the Norfolk pine, coconut palms and philodendron of the Florida countryside, then over the dirt road leading past the front of the two-story house.

Jake's jeep is parked in the driveway. Miami sits like a jewel in the distance.

The tiny model flits around the house and through the back window.

INT. UPPER ROOM

Jake maneuvers the remote knob and suddenly Mark is gazing at himself in the monitor. He lifts his head and the quiet chopper is an inch from his nose.

JAKE
Silent. Invisible to radar...

It darts out the window and disappears into the blue sky.

JAKE (O.S.) (CONT'D)
... And as free and quick as a hummingbird.

EXT. ATLANTIC OCEAN NEAR FLORIDA - DAY

A clear, blue sky vaults over a calm, blue ocean. The only sound is the natural movement of the waves.

SUPER: "THE BERMUDA TRIANGLE"

Then: A low RUMBLE, similar to distant thunder. Strange. Unworldly. Slowly crescendos into a sharp, deafening CLAP...

... Cutting abruptly to a mysterious silence, and at that moment...

... A black helicopter bolts from the blue -- suddenly upon us -- as if emerging from a long invisible tunnel.

Small, angular, futuristic. It looks exactly like Jake's miniature model -- only this chopper is real. Strangely, the WHOP-WHOP of the rotors is muted.

INT. HUMMINGBIRD HELICOPTER - SAME

KENDALL's anxious hands work the instruments.

A grid appears on her windshield. The seat next to her is empty.

On the far horizon an island jumps into view as the chopper suddenly drops. She is frantic, distraught.

KENDALL (O.S.)
Where's that button?

She pushes it, and brushes her hair back behind black sunglasses that contrast silver Egyptian symbol-of-life (ankh) earrings. She is a lovely 35. Her futuristic clothes, blood-stained.

Below, the sparkling blue ocean appears to glide silently by.

EXT./INT. COAST GUARD CUTTER - DAY

A chubby COAST GUARD OFFICER spots the erratic movements of the silent and swift helicopter. Dumbfounded, he races to the

RADAR ROOM

and rushes to the radar screen. He looks in vain for a blip.

COAST GUARD OFFICER
Where is it? Where is it?

The TECHNICIAN looks at him like he's crazy.

TECHNICIAN
Where's what?

ON THE DECK

The Coast Guard Officer hurries through the door and searches the sky. He sees nothing.

EXT./INT. HUMMINGBIRD HELICOPTER - DAY

Just a few feet below, Florida Bay streaks past at amazing speed.

Kendall lifts her sunglasses slightly, wipes away tears.

She pulls up on the collective pitch lever and suddenly she is a half mile above the water. The Southern coast of Florida ascends on the horizon.

She is now over the everglades, with Miami on the far horizon.

FROM THE EVERGLADES

The chopper silently whisks off into the distance.

EXT. SANDY BEACH - DAY

The blue sky meets a beautiful secluded beach at the horizon.

From ground level, the USA X-1 rocket towers upward, ready to blast off. The gargantuan head of Jake Dekker moves into frame -- ah ha, the rocket is actually a miniature.

Jake lies on his side wearing Levis and NASA cap. He laughs excitedly and makes room for a kneeling 11-year-old boy to join in the fun. He touches something on the rocket.

JAKE
That's it!

Jake jumps up. Holds a megaphone to his mouth. Faces north.

JAKE (CONT'D)
Attention. Clear the launch area.
(facing south)
All scouts clear the launch area.

Mark and about a dozen inner-city scouts in street clothes join Jake. Jake makes annoying emergency siren sounds for effect.

But then Jake spots a small boy (SPORT), who stands apart from the others, looking dejected. The other boys ignore him.

Jake walks over to the boy and squats down, sees the dejection.

JAKE (CONT'D)
Hey sport, I need someone with a strong voice for the count down. How about it?

Jake hands him the megaphone and a comforting smile. Sport returns the smile. Jake leads Sport to a spot on the sand.

At the same time, Jake nods to Mark who nods to a TALL BOY. The Tall Boy -- intense with anticipation -- holds a hand remote in his hand. The remaining boys stand back with Mark.

Jake winks at an expectant Sport.

SPORT
Five-four-three-two-one-zero-Blastoff!

The Tall Boy pushes a big, red button -- FFUSSSH! -- the rocket blasts off.

Jake WHOOPS, and the boys revel in his enthusiasm.

They watch the stage-2 rocket separate and drop to earth while the X-1 continues upward. Finally, it explodes over the ocean.

The boys CHEER when a parachute opens and the small capsule flutters downward. Jake leads the charge into the ocean to recover the capsule. So what if his Levis get wet.

Without warning, a huge Chinook helicopter -- loud and ominous -- descends. Two boys fall on their backs in fear.

The tiny rocket capsule falls in the ocean, but no one notices.

A few boys run scared. Jake grabs them.

JAKE
Whoa! Take it easy. She's one of ours. Isn't she pretty?

Caps fly off, but the boys calm down as the Chinook lands.

Mark looks confused, shaken -- what's this about? Jake shrugs.

Two uniformed airmen approach the group. Jake steps forward. Holds his arms out asking for an explanation.

UNIFORM
Jake Dekker?

Dekker calmly nods. They escort him to the chopper.

JAKE
What's going on?

The silent airmen usher Jake into the chopper and SLAM the door.

INT. MILITARY HALLWAY - DAY

A metal door SLAMS shut and ECHOES.

J. C. WARDLE, a sexless woman with an ambitious stride snatches a paper from the hand of PALMER, her stoic, muscular male aide.

Palmer opens a conference room door for Wardle.

INT. MILITARY CONFERENCE ROOM - CONTINUOUS

Jake Dekker stands casually at attention. Wardle notices the wet Levis and bare feet. She's non-plussed and barks an order.

WARDLE
Sit.

Jake sits. Palmer opens his tablet. Grabs a stylus.

Wardle slumps into her chair, takes a sip from her coffee cup, and eyes Jake like he's the fly and she's the spider.

Jake turns his head sideways, trying to get a view of a file that's stamped "Defense Department - Top Secret." She puts her hand on top of the file.

WARDLE (CONT'D)
I just flew in from the Pentagon so this better be good.

She pulls something from the file while Jake tries for a little charm.

JAKE
What a coincidence. I just flew in from Sandy Beach and --

WARDLE
-- Is this your work?

Wardle tosses a drawing of a helicopter labelled "Hummingbird MG-11" towards Jake.

This subdues him. Wardle allows herself only the briefest of smiles and takes another sip.

JAKE
Yes, I submitted the design to Bates. He rejected it. He wants --

WARDLE
-- The Coast Guard spotted this less than fifty miles from here. In the air.

She waits. Jake is stunned, but calm.

Palmer -- face of stone -- nods to himself, takes notes.

JAKE
Impossible.

WARDLE
Later, two civilians in separate incidents. Thought it was Ironman.

She taps the helicopter drawing with her finger.

WARDLE (CONT'D)
So how did this... get into the sky?

JAKE
It didn't. It would take millions of dollars to manufacture a prototype --

WARDLE
Exactly. So who you working for?

Jake is mystified. Casts a glance Palmer's way for an explanation. Runs a frustrated hand through his hair.

JAKE
... NASA.

WARDLE
Not any more. You're terminated, Dekker, and I'm considering prosecution.

JAKE
The charge?

WARDLE
Espionage.

JAKE
You think I sold the plans to a foreign government?

Wardle stands slowly, glares down at Jake, but he doesn't flinch.

WARDLE
The helicopter is out there. If you're connected with it, you're going down. Unless you come clean.

Jake's eyes narrow.

WARDLE (CONT'D)
I want that birdie. And I want it in twenty-four hours. That is all.

Jake -- violated, confused -- staggers out.

DISSOLVE TO:

EXT. MIAMI STREET - NIGHT

Jake wanders in a daze along the sidewalk. He sits on a bench in front of The Excelsior Hotel. Jake speed dials his cell.

JAKE
Mark, you're late for dinner. Give me a call. We need to talk.

He closes his cell and runs his hands through his hair, deep in thought.

Raising his head, he notices a woman about to cross the street. The woman is CHERICE JOULET, whose earth shaking beauty would register a ten on the Richter Scale.

EXT./INT. LIMO - CONTINUOUS

HENRY VAN PELT, 60, long hair, watches Cherise cross the street. He wears a t-shirt and a cell phone ear piece. A boyish face, he's as exuberant as a boy playing a video game.

VAN PELT
This is gonna be fun.
(smiling)
Now!

A nearby black car SCREECHES onto the street.

EXT. MIAMI STREET

Jake spots the black car as it barrels in on Cherise. He shouts a warning.

She deftly dodges the car and dives to the side, her purse sliding to the gutter.

Jake picks up the purse and steps towards her, but another car races towards her.

INT. LIMO

Van Pelt lightly claps his hands in delight -- a kid that never grew up.

EXT. MIAMI STREET

Cherise races up the street and into a crowd of onlookers. The car drives away.

Just as Jake steps forward, a hand grips his shoulder.

The hand belongs to ADRIAN ELAM, 45, a dark and slender man -- perhaps Middle Eastern -- wearing wire-rim glasses.

ADRIAN

Give me the purse.

Jake eyes Adrian suspiciously. Furrows his brow. Hands Adrian the purse. Adrian relaxes -- relieved.

Jake slings his full fist into Adrian's mid-section. Adrian hunches over, sinks to the ground, gasps for breath.

JAKE

It's not yours.

Jake rips the purse from Adrian -- looks scared -- and races away.

Adrian gasps, lifts an icy stare, removes his iPhone.

INT. LIMO

Van Pelt throws a tantrum, angrily striking his cane repeatedly against the window. It spiders.

INT. PARKING GARAGE - NIGHT

Jake slides into his jeep and shuts the door.

EXT./INT. JAKE'S JEEP - CONTINUOUS

Jake looks in the mirror and the car behind him pulls away. He places the purse on the seat next to him and stares at it. Finally, he opens it.

He finds something wrapped in brown paper. He unwraps it carefully. It is the Eye of Ra.

The four purple sugilite crystals at the top glow. He almost drops the artifact. Reverently, he touches the crystals.

On each of four sides, just below each glowing crystal, a thin metal panel hangs from a single hinge. Jake lifts one of the panels from the bottom. Examines the strange engravings on it.

He gently lifts a panel off its hinge. The sugilite crystals immediately cease to glow.

At once, he notices a car parking right behind him. In it, a FROWNING MAN looks directly at him, then drops his eyes.

Jake, alarmed, purposely drops the thin panel on the car seat and starts his jeep.

EXT. PARKING GARAGE

Across the street, a STOCKY MAN in a Hawaiian shirt speaks into a cell as Jake pulls out of his parking space.

STOCKY
... Green jeep, Florida plates H-U-M-Eleven. Small American flag on the radio antenna.

INT. LIMO

In the back seat, Adrian listens on his iPhone. He sits next to Van Pelt.

ADRIAN
Got it.

He frantically keys the last of the info into his iPhone. Van Pelt, calm now, is the picture of smiling confidence.

VAN PELT
I want a print-out on him. Everything.

ADRIAN
He was headed north --

VAN PELT
-- Relax. He has her purse. He'll find her driver's license.
(taps his ear piece)
I already have someone in the area.

ADRIAN
Why couldn't you just let her hand it off? And then --

VAN PELT
(indignant)
-- She's ambitious. No vision. No sense of my destiny.

Adrian nods. Van Pelt is upbeat again.

VAN PELT (CONT'D)
Besides, this is more fun.

EXT./INT. JAKE'S JEEP - NIGHT

Dekker checks his rear-view mirror. A road map lies on the purse next to him. Cherise's driver's license is in his hand. There are cars behind him.

Continuing down the street, he glances in the mirror again and sees headlights. Street lights reflect off his hood as the car turns down another street. Checks the mirror. A Ford follows.

Jake makes another turn. His road map slides onto the floor. He can't reach it. The Ford behind him makes the same turn.

Down the street. His eyes focus on the mirror, watching the headlights. Unexpectedly, he glimpses a car stopped right in front of him. SLAMS on his brakes; nearly rams the car.

Calmly he backs up and peels into another lane. Checks his mirror. Calculating.

The Ford is right on him. Flashes its lights. Once. Twice.

Jake glances in the mirror and the Ford is gone. Without warning, the Ford overtakes him on the left, then slides towards the side of Jake's car, nearly forcing Jake off the street.

The driver's hand gestures to Jake to pull over.

Jake slows down as if to comply, then accelerates and makes a quick turn onto a wide avenue. He comes to a stop light and pulls into the left-hand turn lane.

He peers in the mirror. The pursuing car is only a hundred feet behind.

The left turn signal light continues red. He shakes his head, knowing he has made a mistake. The Ford is only thirty feet behind him.

Still red. Desperately, he looks for an opening. Jerks his head around. The Ford is practically on top of him.

Red. The pursuing car glides right up next to him.

KENDALL

Damn it, Jake, pull over.

The driver knows his name! Jake reacts by turning into traffic, flashing his lights. Cars SCREECH as he makes his left turn.

The left-turn signal finally turns green, but Kendall cannot follow -- she's trapped in her lane.

Jake turns up an alley, makes another turn, then another. Scrutinizes the mirror -- no one is behind him. Runs his hand through his hair.

Checking the driver's license, he turns onto a

DARK ROAD

that leads to a nearby apartment complex.

EXT. APARTMENT COMPLEX - SAME

Kendall's Ford lunges directly in front of him. He SLAMS on the brakes.

Instantly, Kendall and Jake are both out of their cars. Kendall wears shorts and a t-shirt now.

Jake grabs a crow bar.

Kendall runs directly to Jake, then stops. Seemingly paralyzed by his presence, her eyes fill with tears.

He looks confused.

JAKE
What in Heaven's name do you want?

KENDALL
Oh, Jake.

And she leaps into his arms as if she's known him for years, then pulls back and cups his face in her hands.

KENDALL (CONT'D)
Oh Jake, oh Jake, oh....

Jake freezes. This is too much to process.

KENDALL (CONT'D)
Oh Jake. It's really you.

Still frozen....

Finally, he gently pushes Kendall away. He studies her lovely face. Without her sunglasses, he sees an intelligence in her eyes. In fact, she glows with a natural, lively attractiveness.

JAKE
Look... ah. Why...? What...?

Kendall hushes him by taking his hand. He pulls his hand away.

JAKE (CONT'D)
Who...?

KENDALL
Jake. I'm your wife...

JAKE
Wife?

KENDALL
I know this comes as a surprise.

Jake's face looks like his IQ just dropped 100 points. He grunts something unintelligible.

KENDALL (CONT'D)
Come, we don't have time.

Getting panicky, she makes a move to his car, but he stops her. He has managed to put together an hypothesis.

JAKE
Lady, I think you have me confused with -- I don't have any money --

Kendall is desperate and a bit perturbed.

KENDALL
-- Listen, Dream Boy, you wanted this. It was your idea. Please --

JAKE
-- Dream Boy?

KENDALL
It's a term of endearment.

Jake doesn't want to deal with it. He simply walks back to his jeep. She races after him. She is now in full-scale panic.

KENDALL (CONT'D)
I'll explain later. Everything depends --

She stops when she sees the ancient, six-inch-tall artifact in the jeep. She grabs it jubilantly.

Jake drops the crowbar and wrestles the Eye from Kendall's grasp.

JAKE
That does not belong to you.

GRAY (O.S.)
He's right. It belongs to us.

Jake and Kendall turn to see two men in suits, one gray and one blue. GRAY picks up the crowbar while BLUE opens a switchblade.

The switchblade diverts Jake's attention, giving Gray an opportunity to strike Jake on the arm with the crowbar. The Eye of Ra falls.

He then strikes Jake on the back, sending him to his knees. He is about to strike Jake on the head...

... But Kendall dives at Gray, hindering his swing. It's a glancing blow.

Gray flings Kendall onto the road where she skins her knee. Blue snatches the ancient artifact, and the two suits scramble into the black car and drive off.

Kendall rushes to Jake and kneels next to him.

KENDALL
Did you break anything?

He looks at her like she truly is crazy and falls to one side.

Kendall touches the wound on his forehead. He looks up at her, focuses his eyes.

JAKE
It's been a rotten day.

KENDALL
That it has.

She almost cries, but quickly helps him up, hurries him to his jeep, and pushes him in.

EXT./INT. JAKE'S JEEP - NIGHT

Kendall, angry and distraught, drives the jeep. Jake motions back towards the apartment building.

JAKE
What about _your_ car? Ya gonna leave it there?

KENDALL
Um, it's not actually technically mine.

JAKE
You stole it?

Jake looks disgusted.

JAKE (CONT'D)
Where are you taking me?

KENDALL
Home.

JAKE
Do you think we could stop off at the police station on the way?

KENDALL
We're going to your secret hide-away. No mail-man, no sales-man, no meter-man.

Jake double-takes; he's mystified.

She peers over at him -- her anger softens -- and she is suddenly dreamy and vulnerable. She touches his face as if recalling an old memory.

KENDALL (CONT'D)
We meet this Saturday, you know.

JAKE
Where?

KENDALL
If I tell you, you'll get nervous and screw it up.

JAKE
(not buying her story)
We can only hope.

KENDALL
I shouldn't even have mentioned Saturday.

She hits the steering wheel, mad at herself.

Jake examines her face in the lamplight flickering through the jeep window, shakes his head, shuts his eyes.

INT. JAKE'S HOUSE - UPPER ROOM - NIGHT

Jake sits at his desk gingerly touching his head. Kendall enters with an ice pack and Jake notices the blood on her knee.

JAKE
Come here.

IN THE BATHROOM

Kendall sits on the toilet lid. Jake opens the bottom drawer.

KENDALL
We don't have time for this.
(pointing)
Second drawer down.

He shuts the bottom drawer and opens the second drawer. He pulls out the First Aid Kit.

She raises her self-satisfied grin for him to behold.

He grabs the hydrogen peroxide and pours some on her leg.

KENDALL (CONT'D)
Ow, that stings!

Encouraged, Jake pours on some more for good measure. Now it's his turn for a self-satisfied grin.

He rips open a gauze pad and lays it on her leg.

KENDALL (CONT'D)
Jake, I need you to believe me. My name is Doctor Kendall Dekker. I'm an archeologist and we've been married for ten years.

JAKE
Lady, you're nuts!

KENDALL
Then how did I know where the First Aid Kit was -- huh? Or the house?

She throws her hands in the air. Gotcha.

JAKE
So how --

KENDALL
-- I found out from Mark, but I had to be sneaky because I haven't met you yet.

Jake squints, processing.

KENDALL (CONT'D)
Jake, this is serious. Lives are at stake. Now promise you won't interrupt.

Her intensity sobers him. He goes along.

JAKE
Okay. I promise.

Jake tapes the gauze pad to Kendall's leg. She tries to recall.

KENDALL
You're a leader of inner city scouts. They all become fine young men... except Tommy. I believe you still have that condo on Avocado Drive. And before you met me, you were afraid of women.

Jake wants to interrupt, but stops himself.

KENDALL (CONT'D)
See there. You wanted to interrupt me, but you didn't because you made a promise.
(imitating Jake's voice)
And when Jake Dekker makes a promise, he keeps it.
(her own voice)
And I really like that.

Jake gestures that the first aid job is done. Together they walk from the bathroom into

THE UPPER ROOM

where Jake grabs the ice pack and places it on his head. He shows her the chair and she sits in it.

KENDALL
You work for NASA. But your dream is to someday build the Hummingbird MG-Eleven helicopter.

Jake becomes solemn. She's right on. He listens intently.

KENDALL (O.S.) (CONT'D)
Defense department rejected your plans -- the ones on your desk right now -- but things change, Dream Boy, and guess what?

She's happy for him.

KENDALL (CONT'D)
... You get to build it.

Her speech over, she gazes hopefully at Jake.

JAKE
Well Kendall, tell Wardle or whoever sent you I didn't build it, and I didn't sell the design to another country.

Kendall stands. The growing frustration overcomes her. She breaks down into angry tears.

KENDALL
You have no idea what I've been through. How much I love you. How much is at stake.

Jake eyes her suspiciously, won't let her hug him, and holds her at arm's length.

JAKE
Okay, let's assume you're right. How did you get here? From the future, I mean.

KENDALL
I followed the coordinates you give me ten years from now. And then I fly -- flew through the Window... in a Hummingbird MG-Eleven.

He turns away from her. She's making too much sense.

An idea occurs to her -- she removes something from her pocket, spins Jake around, and drops something in his hand.

KENDALL (CONT'D)
I almost forgot. The key.

The key is about two inches long and a quarter-inch wide. It's made of a clear, bluish crystal and contains a long, metallic strand. A metal casing on one end makes the crystal easy to grasp. The other end pyramids to a point.

Jake is astounded. He hurries to his desk, turns to a design of the exact same object and compares the crystal shaft.

JAKE
Okay, then show it to me. Where is it?

KENDALL
Gone.

JAKE
How convenient.

He turns to her. Paces a moment. Assimilating. Then stops.

He holds her shoulders, studies her face intently, his mind racing. She wipes her eyes.

JAKE (CONT'D)
Well, someone saw you fly it. And now the military -- and the police by now -- are after me. They think _I_ built it.

She grabs both of his cheeks playfully.

KENDALL
You did build it.

For the first time, the two smile together.

She embraces him. He does not resist her this time; instead, he comforts her. Runs his hand once through her hair.

He then pulls back and looks at her anew, tries to make her feel better.

JAKE
I'll try to look my best on Saturday.

KENDALL
(with renewed urgency)
Meantime, we must find the Eye of Ra.

Jake removes the Eye of Ra panel from his back pocket and hands it to her. She looks at him dumbfounded.

JAKE
That's part of the Eye. I hid it in the passenger seat of the jeep.

Kendall is suddenly joyful.

KENDALL
Thank Heavens. But they'll be looking for it --

JAKE
Who's they?

KENDALL
(ain't it obvious?)
Thc bad guys.

Jake looks annoyed by her clever little joke.

JAKE
So the "bad guys" will be looking for it. Wait! That gives me an idea. Keep talking.

He takes Kendall's hand, and they hustle out the door.

INT. PENTHOUSE - NIGHT

A sprawling luxury office. Van Pelt looks tired. Adrian pounds on his laptop. A door opens and Van Pelt perks up.

Gray enters, but before he can report, Van Pelt strips away the Eye of Ra he's carrying and excitedly examines it. He freezes when he finds the panel is missing.

VAN PELT
Adrian.

Adrian sees that the panel is missing. Gray looks worried.

GRAY
Isn't that what you wanted?

Van Pelt angrily STRIKES him with his cane. He YELPS.

Adrian returns to his computer printer and glances at the printout. Animated by what he sees, he nods at Van Pelt, who steps around an ailing Gray and quickly joins Adrian.

INT. JAKE'S GARAGE - CONTINUOUS

A single light bulb illuminates the garage. Jake scavenges through a bin of scrap metal. He selects a couple of pieces.

ADRIAN (V.O.)
The man's name is Jake Dekker.

Dekker sets the original Eye of Ra panel on a work bench.

VAN PELT (V.O.)
And he has the missing panel.

Kendall talks to Jake and watches him grind and sand a replica Eye of Ra panel.

ADRIAN (V.O.)
Five years Defense Department. NASA.

INT. PENTHOUSE

Van Pelt is startled.

VAN PELT
They're on to this? We've got to get that panel or there's no time travel. And I wanna time travel.

Eyes glow in the old man's sweet face.

INT. JAKE'S GARAGE

Kendall directs Jake, who engraves some ancient characters on the replica. The characters do not match those on the original.

ADRIAN (V.O.)
Engineer. Loner type. Condo in Miami. On Avocado.

INT. PENTHOUSE

Van Pelt holds the Eye -- minus the panel -- in one hand, and places his other around Adrian. There is a genuine bond between these two.

VAN PELT
Hit the condo. And move fast. Oh, and stream it to me. I wanna watch.

INT. JAKE'S CONDO - NIGHT

With his iPhone, Adrian scans photographs of Jake and Mark, Jake at Cape Canaveral, and others. He stands next to the coffee table, which has been turned upside down. He videos everything via his iPhone.

Gray searches for the missing panel in his own destructive way. Blue moves through the living room with an expensive metal detector.

Gray makes his way to Jake's bedroom. Scowls at a large pictorial of the history of helicopters on the wall. Jerks it from the wall. Sees nothing behind it. Frustrated, he throws it on the floor. It SHATTERS into a thousand pieces.

INT. JAKE'S HOUSE - UPPER ROOM - NIGHT

Jake turns on his arching desk lamp. He lays the two panels on the desk. They examine both panels.

JAKE
A poor imitation, but they might not notice. At least at first.

Kendall touches his arm, gets his attention.

KENDALL
Jake, in a week a computer virus will take control of all military computers. Our own weapons....
(steels herself)
Nuclear bombs explode along the East Coast. It changes everything. Our government. Our way of life.

Jake almost collapses into his chair with the news.

JAKE
You see this happen?

She shakes her head.

KENDALL
It can't happen until they go into the future for the computer virus. They haven't done that yet. That's why we have to get --

Jake stands with a flourish and uses dramatic gestures as he mocks her story.

JAKE
-- So this is all conjecture.
(MORE)

JAKE (CONT'D)
The "bad guys" go to the future, come back with a mystery virus that even McAfee can't remove, and take over the world with it. What bozo came up with that conclusion?

KENDALL
You. You discover the "grand design...," Bozo.

He points to himself. She nods "yes" emphatically. He collapses into his chair again.

JAKE
But "grand design" of what? Could be a computer game -- Super Mario Is the Bomb... literally.

KENDALL
That attack on the road wasn't for a video game.

JAKE
(to himself)
... Nor was the attempted murder of that Cherise lady.

KENDALL
Jake, imagine computer technology ten years from now.
(touches his arm)
They use the Eye to travel through time to use that technology in the present -- next week.

She looks exhausted.

JAKE
So uh... what do I look like in ten years.

Her eyes involuntarily roam to his hairline.

JAKE (CONT'D)
Dang, I lose my hair, don't I?

KENDALL
Nooooooo.

JAKE
(hopefully)
I don't?

KENDALL
Not all of it.

JAKE
I knew it. My dad looked like a walking street lamp.
(a moment of grief; then curiosity)
So in the future, does NASA send men to Mars?

KENDALL
No. And they don't send any women either.

JAKE
Do they find a cure for cancer?

KENDALL
No, but the Cubs win the World Series.

JAKE
Well, that's something. And it's a lot easier to swallow than this "grand design" thing.
(completely serious)
Kendall, no one's going to believe us. The military. The police.

She knows. She takes his hand.

KENDALL
It's just you and me, Dream Boy.

She lays her head on his shoulder. He strokes her hair.

JAKE
So uh... who's the next president?

EXT. TROPICAL PARK - DAY

Palm trees and vacant paths.

Adrian sits on a bench punching his iPhone which is supported by a briefcase on his lap. He is gaming.

Cherise approaches. She speaks with a slight French accent throughout.

CHERISE
Where is Van Pelt?

He glances up, then quickly down at his game.

CHERISE (CONT'D)
Who's winning?

He pockets the iPhone.

ADRIAN
You know he can't be seen with you in public.

CHERISE
(indicating the briefcase)
You couldn't kill me, so now you're going to pay me off?

He sits down on the bench and she sits beside him. He places the briefcase between them.

ADRIAN
It was a mistake in judgment. Our apologies.

CHERISE
Keep the money. I want to be part of the organization. I want in. After all, I _am_ the best at my art.

Adrian assimilates this.

ADRIAN
And Cherise, my dear, your art is needed once again.

Cherise looks at him expectantly.

ADRIAN (CONT'D)
We appreciate your cooperation in acquiring the Eye of Ra, but a panel is missing from it.

CHERISE
And you want me to find it.

INT. UPPER ROOM - DAY

Kendall sits against the wall next to the window. Jake stands next to her gazing through the window to the orange grove below.

KENDALL
Yes, your little sister finally gets married... and to a nice man.

She pours through one of several books and jots things on a yellow pad. Her hair shines with newness.

JAKE
So when does the economy bounce back?

KENDALL
Can we hold the questions of the future for awhile? I'm trying to translate here.

She looks intently at the real Eye of Ra panel.

KENDALL (CONT'D)
Oh, these glyphs go way back, and my Egyptian is rusty.

Jake squats down next to her, anticipating.

KENDALL (CONT'D)
Okay. It says it's a copy of an even earlier Antlantean record.

JAKE
Atlantis?

Kendall returns to her reading.

KENDALL
A window... in time. Here it is!

JAKE
Go on.

KENDALL
A portal -- opening -- that can take you to another time. Okay. Okay.

Her voice rises.

KENDALL (CONT'D)
Atlantis couldn't have been too far away. Look at the coordinates.

She writes, rips out the yellow paper, folds it, and stuffs it in the back of a drawer.

KENDALL (CONT'D)
Hang onto this. You give it to me ten years from now.

Jake shakes his head in wonder. The truth is just too bizarre. And then he gazes at Kendall in admiration.

She writes in a fever.

JAKE
Not too fast. This is not a race.

But she's in a flow. Jake watches her in wonder.

She examines the translation and hastily pages through a book. Suddenly, Kendall stops.

KENDALL
Definitely the Eye of Ra.

JAKE
Hold it. Exactly what is the Eye of Ra?

KENDALL
The Eye of God. In Greek, Photizo. In Latin, Illuminato. In Atlantean, don't know.
(clicks her pen against her lips)
It says that with the Eye you can go to any time. Any place. All you need are coordinates to the Window. And they're written here.

She points at the panel.

KENDALL (CONT'D)
And here.

She opens and closes the drawer where she stuffed the folded yellow paper containing the coordinates.

JAKE
So with the Eye I can pass through the window whenever I want and travel to any place I want, past or future. That glowing Eye can see to any place or time.

Kendall nods.

KENDALL
Some powerful ancient technology. Registers human consciousness. Responds to human will. Whoever possesses it, in effect, controls time.

JAKE
Dang, we could start a church with that thing.

KENDALL
(solemnly)
... Or end the world

JAKE
But you didn't have the Eye. How did you get here?

KENDALL
I had the coordinates you gave me. I could still enter the window, but at risk. And only at certain times in the lunar cycle.
(touching him)
Without the Eye, the window is ten years long. That's what's natural.

Jake steps onto the window sill. He's framed by the window.

JAKE
So, with the coordinates, I'll pass through a window and drop out at the same place, only ten years later.

KENDALL
... If you don't get lost in time.

JAKE
Well, since they don't have the coordinates, we can destroy this panel and their game is over.

Jake holds his hands up and smiles proudly.

KENDALL
But the coordinates are written on all four panels. We can only hope thcy don't realize yet that they have them. Or can't translate them.

Kendall lets Jake assimilate this. Then he comes to a realization.

JAKE
Wait a minute, this looks Masonic.

Jake removes a one dollar bill from his billfold. He taps his finger repeatedly on the pyramid and the all-seeing eye.

JAKE (CONT'D)
Maybe the Eye of Ra is the same as the All-seeing Eye.

Jake points at a slogan on the dollar bill.

JAKE (CONT'D)
What does that mean?

KENDALL
Novus ordo seclorum? New order of the ages.

She stands and paces.

JAKE
New world order.

KENDALL
That's the "grand design." After the devastation, we will... ah, we would have a new world government. But it's not what you'd hope for.

JAKE
That means that whoever is behind the computer virus heads this group.

KENDALL
They'll blackmail governments.

Jake pulls the fake Eye of Ra panel out of his back pocket. He opens a drawer, grabs a few miniscule metal objects, sticks one on the panel and drops the others in his pocket.

JAKE
A tracking beacon.
(sighs)
Well, guess I'm the bait.

KENDALL
You just be careful. You get yourself killed and ten years together gets flushed.

INT. JAKE'S CONDO - DAY

Jake enters his ransacked condo. Looks around. Picks up the shattered picture of himself, Mark, and his inner city boys.

Finally, he steps through the doorway.

EXT. JAKE'S CONDO - CONTINUOUS

Jake strolls to his parking space and stops. There in his jeep sits the gorgeous Cherise Joulet.

CHERISE
I was hoping this was yours.

JAKE
Aren't you the lady who lost the purse?

CHERISE
Yes, and you were jumped trying to return it. I watched from my apartment window. In fact, I wanted to thank you. May I buy you lunch?

INT. SURVEILLANCE VAN - CONTINUOUS

Wardle sits next to Palmer while two other agents -- one wearing a RED VEST over his t-shirt and the other a BALL CAP -- operate the electronic equipment. They listen to Jake and Cherise.

JAKE (V.O.)
Sure, I could use a bite.

WARDLE
Follow, but do not get too close.

Red Vest jumps up to the driver's seat. Ball Cap checks the clip in his Uzi.

WARDLE (CONT'D)
(to Ball Cap)
This is surveillance only.
(to Palmer)
What do we have on the girl? She looks familiar.

EXT. JAKE'S CONDO COMPLEX - CONTINUOUS

Jake and Cherise pull out of the parking lot onto Avocado Drive.

He is soon followed by the van.

INT. CARIBBEAN RESTAURANT DAY

Cherise smiles her charming smile. The faint sounds of a steel drum band can be heard.

JAKE
So how did you find me?

CHERISE
There was a woman with you who left her car. Your address was there.

EXT. CARIBBEAN RESTAURANT - SAME

On the side walk, the steel drum band plays.

Some distance from the band, Red Vest places a tiny listening device on the restaurant window nearest Jake and Cherise.

INT. CARIBBEAN RESTAURANT

JAKE
You were lucky. I'm not there very much.

CHERISE
You're right. I am lucky. The guy who clubbed you? They caught him. So I got the... package.

INT. SURVEILLANCE VAN

Wardle is into the flow. She nods at Palmer.

WARDLE
"Package."

JAKE (V.O.)
So everything's cool.

Another affirmative nod from Wardle. She's got Jake where she wants him.

EXT. CARIBBEAN RESTAURANT

Red Vest pretends to enjoy the steel drum band. He glances at Wardle's van, which is parked across the street next to a parking structure.

INT. SURVEILLANCE VAN

Wardle speaks into a mic.

WARDLE
Keep an eye out for anyone else suspicious looking.

EXT. CARIBBEAN RESTAURANT

Red Vest listens through his earphone. He turns to a tense Ball Cap who is next to a green car.

INT. SURVEILLANCE VAN

Wardle turns to Palmer.

WARDLE
Let's get some back-up, just in case they split up.

EXT. CARIBBEAN RESTAURANT

Ball Cap, who also wears an earpiece, approaches Red Vest.

BALL CAP
Anything abnormal?

Red Vest shakes his head "no." He pushes his palm down, as if to tell Ball Cap to relax. Ball Cap acknowledges.

INT. CARIBBEAN RESTAURANT - LATER

Jake and Cherise laugh together. She signs the credit slip.

JAKE
Aren't the inscriptions in some kind of hieroglyphics?

CHERISE
Of some sort.

JAKE
Well, what do they say?

Jake listens carefully.

CHERISE
Just a list of genealogies. Book of Breathings. But it's worth a lot of money. That's why a few unsavory types are after it.

INT. SURVEILLANCE VAN

Wardle looks confused.

WARDLE
They're talking code. What unsavory types? Get a copy to Cryptology.

EXT. CARIBBEAN RESTAURANT

Ball Cap stands stiffly by the entrance. Red Vest is still "enjoying" the steel drum band.

A yellow cab pulls up to the curb in front of the restaurant.

INT. SURVEILLANCE VAN

Wardle watches with anticipation.

WARDLE
Here they come. Where's that backup?

Palmer shows Wardle an image on his tablet. Wardle looks at it -- then shoots a surprised look at Palmer. She speaks to her agents.

WARDLE (CONT'D)
Careful. The woman is Patty Jacobs. The terrorist.

Ball Cap touches his earpiece. He looks twitchy. Red Vest lounges near the green car.

EXT. CARIBBEAN RESTAURANT

Jake opens the door for Cherise.

CHERISE
Anyway, there still is a piece missing from the pyramid.

She sees Ball Cap a few yards away, his back towards her -- she spots the earphone.

As she and Jake walk, she scans the area. Speaks softly.

CHERISE (CONT'D)
Jake, see the van across the street?

Jake spots the van.

CHERISE (CONT'D)
The guy in the red vest by the green car. And the man here?

Jake notices them both.

CHERISE (CONT'D)
Just do what I say.

JAKE
What are you talking about?

But he calmly appraises the situation while she approaches Ball Cap directly.

CHERISE
Have an Uzi I can borrow?

Her stare prompts him to reach for his Uzi.

From inside her sleeve, a knife flicks into her hand. It slashes across Ball Cap's throat. This confirms that Cherise was the "thief" who stole the Eye of Ra in the first place.

Jake is sickened and stunned by the sight. He lays the tips of his fingers against his head and controls himself.

The steel drum band stops playing.

Cherise's other hand pushes Ball Cap's Uzi to the side as it fires across the abandoned steel drums, sounding out an odd staccato tune.

The nearby not-so-bright CABBIE ducks and is not hit. He rolls out of the cab and cowers behind a stunned but angry Jake.

CABBIE
What the hell is going on?

JAKE
I'm dating Lara Croft; what's it look like?

CABBIE
Lara Croft, the tomb raider?

Meanwhile, Cherise slices Ball Cap's hand and the Uzi drops. She turns him around as Red Vest springs into action, but he can't fire at Cherise while Ball Cap is used as a shield.

Cherise drops to the ground, rolls over to the Uzi, picks it up, and ducks behind the cab near Jake.

Ball Cap crumbles to the ground, bleeding out.

SPRANG! A stray hits the cab fender. The petrified Cabbie utters an expletive.

INT. SURVEILLANCE VAN

Wardle is infuriated.

WARDLE
Shit. There goes our cover.
Now we have to arrest them.
(to Red Vest)
Hold your ground. Help is coming.

EXT. CARIBBEAN RESTAURANT - BEHIND THE GREEN CAR

Red Vest hears in his earphone and nods.

BEHIND THE CAB

Jake assesses the situation.

JAKE
Lady, this isn't my fight.

Cherise spots Palmer's head behind the van.

CHERISE
Stay down!

But Jakes rises, his arms flung in the air.

JAKE
I surrender! Don't shoot!

A bullet SHATTERS the plate glass behind him. Jake drops like a sack of sand beside the Cabbie.

JAKE (CONT'D)
What's happened to manners in this country?

The Cabbie is now nestled in the gutter, occasionally glancing up. He sticks his thumb in his mouth.

Cherise throws her car keys at Jake.

CHERISE
Red Vette. Level Two. Go get it.

Jake throws the keys back.

JAKE
I'm not running across there.

She peers suspiciously at a black car cruising slowly down the street.

CHERISE
You're right. Into the cab.

She shoves the hot muzzle of the Uzi into the terrified Cabbie's throat. The Cabbie opens the door and crawls inside as Jake and Cherise crawl into the back.

The shooting stops.

INSIDE THE CAB

Cherise threatens the already shell-shocked Cabbie with her Uzi. Jakes moves her Uzi away and handles the situation his way. He speaks gently; the Cabbie is grateful.

JAKE
Into the parking structure. Safest bet. Go.

SURVEILLANCE VAN

Wardle watches the cab peel out.

WARDLE
They're in the cab. Shoot out the tires. Take care you don't hit the cab driver.

The cab peels out and races directly across the street towards the parking structure.

FROM THE GREEN CAR

Red Vest fires at the cab's tires, hitting one. But the cab races up the parking structure ramp.

The black car follows in pursuit.

IN THE CAB

Cherise's smile betrays an icy confidence.

CHERISE
(to cabbie)
You're doing great. Now when you reach level two, stop, and let us out. And then, keep going, as fast as you can to the top.

The Cabbie glances at Jake for confirmation. Jake nods.

The black car enters just as they round their first turn.

EXT. PARKING STRUCTURE

The van moves in front of the structure exit, blocking passage.

Wardle jumps out of the van, hollers to Palmer.

WARDLE
Take the other exit.

Palmer races away.

Wardle hears SIRENS, looks across the street at the gawkers. Her countenance shows genuine sadness at the sight of Ball Cap on thc ground.

Quickly she places an earpiece in her ear.

INT. PARKING STRUCTURE

The cab rounds a corner, quickly brakes. Jake and Cherise roll out and duck behind the red Vette. The cab continues.

Almost immediately, the black car races past in pursuit.

Cherise is cocky.

CHERISE
Okay, you're driving.

JAKE
(making up an excuse)
But my license has expired.

She waves the Uzi at him. Jake steps into the driver's seat. His face reflects a growing anger.

EXT. TOP OF PARKING STRUCTURE

The cab stops and the black car immediately pulls alongside. A BLACK AGENT jumps out with gun trained on the cab, but only the Cabbie steps out, hands held high.

The agent checks the car and speaks into a thumb mic.

BLACK AGENT
Not in the cab.

EXT. PARKING STRUCTURE - WARDLE'S EXIT

Wardle hears and smiles, her van still blocking the exit.

WARDLE
Palmer. They're on their way down. Watch for the jeep.

She glances across the street. Paramedics and police have arrived.

PALMER'S EXIT

Palmer watches the red Vette slowly descend. Palmer sees only one male driver and relaxes, but holds out his palm to stop the car anyway. With the other, he holds out his ID.

EXT./INT. RED VETTE

Jake continues to drive. He controls his anger and fear.

JAKE
A man is asking me to stop.

Cherise is hiding on the passanger seat floor.

CHERISE
Does he have a gun?

JAKE
Not in his hand.

CHERISE
Well, I do. So we're home free.

JAKE
Don't shoot him. Leave it to me.

Cherise looks impressed.

PALMER'S EXIT

Palmer watches the red Vette slow. Suddenly, it peels out and heads directly at him. Flashes bright lights.

Palmer drops his ID, reaches for his gun, but the speeding Vette speads towards him. He dives out of the way.

When the Vette passes, he finally pulls out his gun, but it's too late.

Palmer speaks into his thumb mic.

PALMER
They got through. Headed west on Fifth.

WARDLE'S EXIT

Wardle's shoulders droop. She swears to herself.

WARDLE
Home base, do you copy that?

INT. RED VETTE

Cherise is satisfied.

CHERISE
Step on it.

Jake steps on it, but his face is a mask of steely anger.

EXT. WARDLE'S EXIT

Wardle sadly watches the paramedics load Ball Cap into the ambulance. The flashing red light turns off. She's mad now.

WARDLE
Now that we know he's dealing with a known terrorist, he becomes expendable.

EXT. STREET - LATER

The red Vette races down a street.

INT. RED VETTE

Cherise looks back through the rear windshield. She signals a turn. Jake turns down an alley.

CHERISE
Stop. Turn out the lights.

He stops and turns out his lights. She steps outside and then gets back into the front seat. Without hesitating, she moves over to him, kisses him on the cheek as if to thank him.

She examines his face. He looks emotionless, but anger simmers underneath.

JAKE
Pretty handy with a knife....

CHERISE
They think I have the missing panel.
(feigned reluctance)
They don't realize I'm C.I.A.

She removes her ID. It looks official.

He softens somewhat, allows himself a cynical smile.

CHERISE (CONT'D)
That pyramid is more valuable than I let on, Jake. There are terrorists after it.

JAKE
The bad guys.

CHERISE
It has certain properties.

Before Jake can speak:

CHERISE (CONT'D)
It's classified. But your life is in danger because -- well -- you're the only person who could have that missing panel.

She watches his eyes. His smile is warm.

JAKE
I didn't realize I had it till last night. And after our delightful lunch, I'm glad to get rid of it.

He removes the fake Eye of Ra panel from his pants pocket and hands it to her.

The beauty collapses in his arms -- relieved.

JAKE (CONT'D)
The whole idea was to get it back to you. I'm just glad this is over.

And he gives her a peck on the cheek. She likes the gesture.

CHERISE
I don't think we should return to the parking structure right now. Can I drop you off someplace?

EXT. A MALL - LATER

Jake steps out of the Vette and Cherise drives away. Jake looks around until a white Smart Car pulls up. He scratches his head.

EXT./INT. SMART CAR

Kendall, the driver, holds Jake's custom iPad mini on her lap. He gets in.

JAKE
You couldn't take the bus? Or a cab? As we discussed.

KENDALL
It was just sitting there with the engine running, so.... At least it's cozy.

JAKE
The police will --

KENDALL
-- I switched the plates.

She taps her head to indicate how smart she is.

KENDALL (CONT'D)
Been waiting forever.
(hands over the iPad)
I wasn't expecting a red Vette with a bimbo inside. What happened to your jeep?

JAKE
(reluctantly)
Impounded by now.

KENDALL
Oh! And so now we need a car.

Vindicated, she taps the dash victoriously.

Jake drops his head and blinks on the iPad screen. He sees a moving blue dot and hides his smile from Kendall.

JAKE
(teasing)
She's no bimbo. Oh no. And she's dangerous... in more ways than one.

KENDALL
What's that supposed to mean?

JAKE
She kissed me. But not on the lips. It was only our first date.

Kendall slowly moves in for a kiss. Jake's eyes grow wide.

KENDALL
How would you like one on the lips?

Jake leans towards her and closes his eyes. Anticipating.

Just as she is about to kiss him....

KENDALL (CONT'D)
Mmmmmmmm -- maybe later. If you're nice.

Jake looks devastated. Kendall looks satisfied -- Gotcha.

KENDALL (CONT'D)
Come on, Dream Boy, let's see where this "dangerous woman" takes us.

INT. RED VETTE - DAY

While driving, the "dangerous woman" pulls a cell phone from her purse and punches a number.

CHERISE
I have the panel. This time no fancy hand-offs on street corners. Bring me in.

She hangs up and looks very satisfied with herself.

INT. SMART CAR - DAY

Jake watches the blue dot on the iPad mini. He taps the screen twice, and a compass layout and grid appear.

JAKE
Make a right.

Jake breathes a deep SIGH, as if exhaling the horrors at the restaurant.

EXT. HVP BUILDING - DAY

Cherise drives into the "HVP International" parking structure.

INT. SMART CAR

Jake checks the compass layout on the screen. The blue dot has moved closer to the center of the screen.

JAKE
I think we've found the viper's nest.

INT. HVP BUILDING - CONFERENCE ROOM

Van Pelt and Adrian sit around the table. Van Pelt lays his cane across the conference table. Gray and Cherise enter the room.

There is a moment of eerie silence as Cherise sizes up the long-haired Van Pelt and his eyes roam over her body.

CHERISE
It's a pleasure to meet you at last, Mr. Van Pelt.

No hands are extended, however, and Cherise sits down.

VAN PELT
(lusting)
Why don't you begin by showing us what you have. Referring to the panel, of course.

Cherise removes the Eye of Ra panel from her purse.

Van Pelt lightly claps his hands in unbridled delight.

EXT./INT. SMART CAR

Kendall parks on the street a short distance from the building.

The blue dot is now practically at center. Jake looks up at the building. He works furiously at the keyboard, creating a vertical metric grid.

KENDALL
How much do you bet it's the penthouse?

Jake strikes "Enter" and the blue dot appears high on the vertical grid.

JAKE
You should have kissed me when you had the chance. Now you'll have to wait 'til Saturday.

He winks.

KENDALL
Of course, I already know what it's like. I have ten years experience. You'll just have to wonder.

He responds with a "touche" smile.

A pause and he nods -- this is her cue. She races out of the car. His eyes follow her. He touches his lips.

INT. HVP BUILDING - CONFERENCE ROOM

Van Pelt hands the panel to Adrian who begins his study.

CHERISE
As I mentioned to Adrian, I wish to add my talents to the organization.

VAN PELT
Freelance business dropping off?

CHERISE
On the contrary. I just want a secure future in my old age, and I believe you are the future.

Van Pelt warms up to this acknowledgment.

VAN PELT
Oh, you're starting to get the vision?
(and then coldly)
We'll call you.

Cherise takes that as her signal to leave.

VAN PELT (CONT'D)
Just a minute.

Cherise turns to face him. He's suddenly beaming.

VAN PELT (CONT'D)
If you cross me, I'll kill you. I'm everywhere.

CHERISE
If I must prove my loyalty, I will.

She smiles at him seductively. Van Pelt likes that -- his baby face glows.

Cherise turns to exit while Adrian examines the panel with a jeweler's loupe.

ADRIAN
Stop her.

Van Pelt nods to Gray. Gray grabs Cherise before she exits, but she easily shakes him.

ADRIAN (CONT'D)
There is something wrong with this panel.

He waits for a response. Van Pelt picks up his cane.

ADRIAN (CONT'D)
It's a forgery.

CHERISE
(dumbstruck)
He gave me a fake?

Van Pelt slams his cane against the table.

VAN PELT
And you want to add your "talents" to the organization?

CHERISE
He had to know he was giving me a fake. That means he has the original.

VAN PELT
(tapping his cane)
But it's of no use to him. If he was going to sell it, he would have sold it by now.

CHERISE
Maybe it's the Eye itself he wants.

This makes sense to everyone.

VAN PELT
Well, he just signed his own death warrant.

Van Pelt puts an arm around Cherise. He's creepy.

VAN PELT (CONT'D)
You want to prove your loyalty? Bring me the panel. The real one this time.
(tapping his cane)
And then destroy the evidence. And please record it.
(a childish smile)
I wanna watch.

EXT. HVP BUILDING

Kendall stands on a sidewalk. She carefully watches one of the parking exits. Her eyes then shift to the building entrance, then back to the parking exit.

AT THE OTHER END OF THE BUILDING

Jake watches another parking exit.

BACK TO KENDALL

who sees the red Vette exit. Kendall races back to Jake.

INT. SMART CAR

Kendall jumps in.

KENDALL
She just drove away.

Jake looks down at his custom iPad and the blue dot remains constant. He nudges Kendall good-naturedly.

JAKE
You were right. The penthouse suite.

KENDALL
We need to get up there and scout the place. Get a name.

The iPad blinks off.

JAKE
Well, there are two problems with me going up there. First, they might recognize me. By now, they know who I am. Second, if I'm killed I won't meet you this Saturday and you'll be robbed of ten years of glorious blissful marriage.

KENDALL
I hate to miss the "glorious blissful" part. What exactly do you have in mind?

Kendall looks at him suspiciously. Her face has very little make-up.

INT. HVP BUILDING - PENTHOUSE - LATER

Make-up -- Kendall's face is now loaded with it.

She poses as a stripper gyrating to the music playing on her iPod and dock.

Van Pelt is delighted. Adrian is wary. The RECEPTIONIST is nervous.

As Kendall dances, she notices Jake's mini-helicopter rise outside the window. She frowns. She turns and shakes her booty that direction.

INTERCUT - SMART CAR/PENTHOUSE

SMART CAR

Jake gapes, mouth open, at the little monitor while turning up the sound on his iPad.

KENDALL (V.O.)
To the Grand Poobah...

PENTHOUSE

KENDALL (CONT'D)
... from your friend, who shall remain nameless. Have a special day.

Off comes the skirt. She wiggles out. Van Pelt is nearly drooling.

Off comes the blouse. He drops his cane.

SMART CAR

Jake has a hand over his eyes, but his fingers are spaced so he can see through.

PENTHOUSE

Kendall struts to the window seductively. Taps the mic on her bra hard twice.

SMART CAR

The tapping results in loud FEEDBACK SOUNDS.

KENDALL (V.O.) (CONT'D)
Just for you.

Jake, in a rush to turn down the sound on his iPad, drops the monitor. He reaches quickly to the floor to retrieve it and bumps his head on the dash.

JAKE
Dang.

PENTHOUSE

Kendall turns abruptly and points her finger at Van Pelt. She glides towards his waiting arms.

VAN PELT
What friend? Who sent you?

KENDALL
It's a secret, Cutie Pie.

She plays the bimbo perfectly. She slips away, but Van Pelt grabs her by the arm. He nods at Adrian who stops the music. She remains unruffled.

KENDALL (CONT'D)
Don't know. He paid cash.

The Receptionist looks uneasy.

Van Pelt puts on a happy face and strokes Kendall's neck. His hand comes perilously close to the tiny mic on her bra.

VAN PELT
I'm sorry...

SMART CAR

Jake looks worried. He listens intently and watches the monitor.

VAN PELT (V.O.) (CONT'D)
... It's just that I'm so busy right now. Let's just call it square... unless you'd like to step into my office.

Concerned, Jake nearly stands and hits his head.

PENTHOUSE

KENDALL
Act-u-ally, I'm due 'cross town. In thirty.

For a moment, it looks like Van Pelt might cry -- vulnerable -- then he angrily gestures to the Receptionist, who looks nervous.

VAN PELT
... Show the bitch out.

He grabs his cane and throws it at nothing in particular. The receptions SQUEALS in fright.

RECEPTIONIST
Yes, Mr. Van Pelt.

SMART CAR

Jake repeats the magic words.

JAKE
Yes, Mr. Van Pelt.

INT. HVP BUILDING - ADRIAN'S OFFICE - A MOMENT LATER

Van Pelt steps in. Adrian scans several security screens. On one they watch Kendall step out of the elevator. On another, she hurries out of the building and into Jake's car.

VAN PELT
There's a man in that car. Got to be Dekker.

Van Pelt smiles -- self-satisfied. Adrian is not thrilled.

VAN PELT (CONT'D)
This is just too fun.

EXT. JAKE'S HOUSE - DAY

Jake steps out of house and sees Cherise in his jeep.

JAKE
You're not stalking me, are you? Tell the truth.

Cherise steps out of the jeep and glides towards him. She has tears in her eyes.

CHERISE
Oh Jake, there is something you should know.

She looks sincerely in love.

CHERISE (CONT'D)
I am your wife... from the future.

Jake is perplexed.

CHERISE (CONT'D)
And... and... you lose all your hair.

She pulls off his wig and he is completely bald. She wails in sorrow.

INT. UNIVERSITY LIBRARY - SAME

Jake awakens with a start! It was just a dream.

He looks down at the drool spot on the library table. Then feels his hair. He sighs in relief.

KENDALL (O.S.)
This is an antique! How do you find anything with it?

She's using his custom iPad mini.

JAKE
Huh? It's cutting edge. Custom. Did the work myself. It's not even on the market yet.

KENDALL
If I'd had time, I would have brought something useful.

She continues to work. He yawns, rubs hands through his hair, making sure his hair is still there.

JAKE
Must've fallen asleep.

KENDALL
I guess watching me dance wore you out.

She gestures him over. He stands behind her and puts his hands on her shoulders. She closes her eyes a moment, enjoying that.

JAKE
His father was a billionaire who died violently. The guy is loaded.

KENDALL
But there's a pattern. He was rejected by his father....

JAKE
So you think he killed him?

KENDALL
... And I read earlier -- while you were sleeping -- that he was left standing at the altar.

JAKE
How do you jilt a billionaire?

KENDALL
Now, this...

A few keystrokes. Jake looks at a newspaper headline. It reads: "Van Pelt's Nomination Defeated. Federal Reserve Chair Remains Empty."

Jake is engrossed.

KENDALL (CONT'D)
Voted down by Congress.

JAKE
The guy's an idiot!

KENDALL
Hardly. One-eighty I.Q. But I'm not done. He was later turned down by the World Monetary Fund Board.

JAKE
The guy can't buy a job.

KENDALL
(proudly)
And last of all, just hours ago, he was rejected by me.

Jake gazes into her eyes.

JAKE
And that will probably send him over the edge.

KENDALL
Ask me, he's already over the edge.

Remembering something, she grabs a piece of paper.

KENDALL (CONT'D)
Here's the layout of the Penthouse as best I remember, but I'm sure you saw it better than I.

She's got him, and Jake likes it. He squeezes her shoulders, chuckles, and then sits down next to her.

KENDALL (CONT'D)
So what's next?

JAKE
There's only one thing we can do.

EXT. HAAGEN-DAZ - DAY

Sitting outside at a table, the two enjoy ice cream cups. They laugh MOS.

LATER

The ice cream is gone. They are seriously working over plans on a yellow pad.

LATER

Kendall glances at the iPad screen and writes something on a dollar bill.

With cell in hand, Jake drops the dollar bill in front of him. There, beside the pyramid and the all-seeing eye is a hand-written phone number.

Kendall scoots her chair close as Jake punches in the numbers.

JAKE
Mr. Henry Van Pelt.

He listens, exchanging nervous glances with Kendall.

JAKE (CONT'D)
Mr. Ra. R-A. As in Eye of Ra.
(nodding to the phone)
He is expecting my call.

Jake breathes deeply, exchanges encouraging looks with Kendall. She squeezes his hand momentarily.

INT. PENTHOUSE

Henry Van Pelt is momentarily stunned by the word "Ra," and then smiles knowingly. The game is on.

VAN PELT
Hot diggity!

He gestures to the anxious Receptionist who nearly runs out.

INTERCUT PHONE CONVERSATION - PENTHOUSE/HAAGEN-DAZ

He picks up the phone and turns on the phone speaker.

VAN PELT
Who is this?

Adrian steps in.

JAKE
Jake Dekker.

VAN PELT
Yes, Jake.

JAKE
I have the piece you are looking for.

Van Pelt is calm. Beads of perspiration appear on Jake's forehead.

VAN PELT
Bring it to --

JAKE
-- It's not free. I want five hundred K. And I don't take American Express.

VAN PELT
Too much.

Jake winks at Kendall -- he takes control.

JAKE
Meet me at Joe's Stone Crab at seven tonight. Just you and the cash.

Van Pelt speaks before Jake can hang up. He looks as happy as a clam at high tide.

VAN PELT
Listen carefully, Jakey-boy, I'll be at Tropical Park tomorrow morning at ten. The gazebo on the lake.
(MORE)

VAN PELT (CONT'D)
I'll pay you what you want. You'll be fabulously wealthy! But the merchandise better be genuine.

Van Pelt hangs up before Jake can speak. He's absolutely joyous. He lightly claps his hands in delight.

VAN PELT (CONT'D)
I want that park saturated.

AT THE HAAGEN-DAZ TABLE

Jake looks disturbed. Pockets his cell. This did not go exactly as planned.

JAKE
Tomorrow. At ten.

Jake runs his fingers through his hair.

KENDALL
Don't worry. We have something they don't.

A playful smile. Jake looks confused....

EXT. JAKE'S HOUSE - DAY

The white Smart Car parks in the driveway. Jake and Kendall step out and walk around the house into the back yard. Together, they enter the orange grove.

JAKE
You lied. You told me it was gone.

IN THE ORANGE GROVE

They walk serenely through the quiet grove.

KENDALL
Sorry. I wanted to wait for the right moment.

Angling to the right and rounding a tree, they step into a small clearing, a meadow.

Then Jake falls to his knees as if beholding a god. His lips tremble.

He stands, takes a few steps, reaches out his hand and touches the black

<u>Hummingbird MG-11 Helicopter</u>.

It is real. The same that was piloted by Kendall from 10 years in the future. The same that Jake is currently designing.

Jake's image reflects in the tinted window, then Kendall's image appears beside him.

He runs his hand through his hair and approaches the door. The door won't open. Kendall hands him the small crystal shaft "key" that opens the door.

He inserts the crystal key into the door lock, jerks the handle and the door CLICKS opens. Reverently, he steps inside.

INT. HUMMINGBIRD HELICOPTER

Jake admires the controls. Kendall steps in from the other side, looking like a mother on Christmas morning.

Above, a large clip holds a faded yellow paper with fold creases on it.

Jake becomes solemn and places his hand to his head.

JAKE
Thank you, Kenny.

Kendall is both surprised and touched that he used her nickname.

KENDALL
Anything for you, Dream Boy.

She's a woman in love.

They buckle up. Jake is both eager and unsure.

JAKE
Well, I built it. I should be able to pilot it. Right?

FROM THE HOUSE

The orange trees stand motionless.

The little black chopper darts suddenly sideways, ripping up a few trees, then jerks awkwardly up, then across.

EXT./INT. HUMMINGBIRD HELICOPTER - DAY

Jake works the controls. Kendall touches his hand on the collective pitch lever.

KENDALL
Easy, it's sensitive.

He tries something else, but both he and Kendall are thrust sideways in their seats. Then straight up at incredible speed.

KENDALL (CONT'D)
Jake, Jake, don't put us in orbit.

But he's WHOOPING and HOLLERING like a teenager.

JAKE
This is great!

Kendall looks terrified as they drop towards an orange grove.

At the last minute Jake avoids a crash and swoops at incredible speed just above the grove.

EXT. ANOTHER GROVE - CONTINUOUS

Workers pick oranges. The MG-11 zips past silently, shaking the oranges from the trees. Two workers high-five each other.

EXT./INT. HUMMINGBIRD HELICOPTER - MINUTES LATER

Jake has calmed down -- the adrenalin rush has run its course, but Kendall looks thrashed. It is near sunset now.

They glide over the beautiful Florida countryside. On the west horizon, an orange-red sunset shoots a beam of red light through the Hummingbird window.

JAKE
Tell me, does the government ever figure out how to use this thing?

KENDALL
It's just one of an entire fleet. Silent. Invisible to radar. And it can out-maneuver anything.

Kendall quickly adds.

KENDALL (CONT'D)
Oh, and it is armed with two missiles.

JAKE
Well, I knew _that_ was inevitable. How did you get it?

KENDALL
I stole it.

JAKE
You stole government property?

KENDALL
You helped me.

As if to say that makes it okay. Jake points to himself, as if that is impossible. She's delighted.

KENDALL (CONT'D)
You change a lot before Saturday.

JAKE
In two days?

EXT. HUMMINGBIRD HELICOPTER

The chopper whisks low along the countryside. Its exterior and interior lights go out.

INT. HUMMINGBIRD HELICOPTER

A strand of beach appears on the horizon.

JAKE
I see two problems. First, the military wants my bird. Gotta stay clear of them and the police.

KENDALL
Second, we must capture the Eye of Ra from Van Pelt. Or worst case --<u>melt it down</u> so no one can use it. It's too powerful. Those are your words.

Kendall looks out at the window and is suddenly sad. She rests her hand on his shoulder a moment. Then puts her hands around his arm.

She looks up at him, admires him.

He keeps his eyes straight ahead. She slides her hand over his knee and starts up his thigh.

And at that moment, he jerks the collective pitch lever sideways.

The chopper suddenly moves sideways, throwing her against the side door.

They both laugh.

EXT. SANDY BEACH - NIGHT

The helicopter silently flits around like a hummingbird.

It hovers a moment near the beach, then slowly drifts along the sea shore, and finally out to sea.

EXT./INT. HUMMINGBIRD HELICOPTER - CONTINUOUS

The two silently watch the sea. Jake takes Kendall's hand. She's surprised. She gives him a look that would melt tempered steel.

KENDALL
People think you are such a stuffed shirt, but you're the most creative, fun, and obnoxious boy scout I know.

JAKE
Trustworthy, loyal --

KENDALL
-- I like loyal.

JAKE
Helpful, friendly --

KENDALL
(seductively)
-- You really could be more friendly, you know.

JAKE
Courteous. Kind. Obedient.

KENDALL
Mmmm, lets work on obedient for awhile.

The chopper turns southward, back down the beach. It's night, and the lights of Miami glow in the distance.

From inside the chopper, Jake and Kendall see Miami slowly drift by on their right.

Jake adjusts several controls and the helicopter begins a slow 360-degree, continuous turn.

With the helicopter interior and exterior lights out, they appear suspended in the air with no helicopter visible.

As they slowly turn, they see a leisurely moon rise on the water, then the long strand of beach, and finally the lights of Miami, then the moon on the water again. Rotating....

JAKE
You know, we should just fly away, Take the time we have now --

KENDALL
(intense)
No. We must capture the Eye.

JAKE
Right now, I just want to capture you.

They kiss, just them forming a silhouette -- just them against the moon.

The moon DISSOLVES into a morning sun.

INT. MARK'S OFFICE - DAY

Mark is busy at his desk when there's a commotion at his door. He looks up as Wardle and Palmer stride in past a nervous SECRETARY. Wardle shows a badge.

WARDLE
Mark James?

Marks starts to rise. Smiles nervously.

MARK
Yes. What's this --

WARDLE
-- Sit.

Mark drops back into his chair. Wardle leans forward.

WARDLE (CONT'D)
We need help finding a friend of yours.

EXT. HVP BUILDING - DAY

In the white Smart Car, Jake (wearing a sports jacket) pulls up to a parking space across from the building. He steps out of the car with a briefcase.

EXT. TROPICAL PARK - CONTINUOUS

Henry Van Pelt sits down by the gazebo -- alone. He looks around for Jake and taps his cane on the ground. He wears his cell phone ear piece.

Nearby, Kendall observes.

EXT. HVP BUILDING

Jake hurries up the steps.

INT. HVP BUILDING - MAIN LOBBY

Jake waves at the WATCHMAN as he walks past. Steps onto an

ELEVATOR

where he punches the "P" for penthouse. Up, up he goes.

He removes his custom iPad mini from his briefcase and taps it deftly with his fingers. The grid format appears, as does the familiar blue dot.

Jake watches the "P" indicator above the elevator door light up. He pockets the iPad. DING -- the elevator doors open. Jake puts on bulky horned-rimmed glasses and steps into the

PENTHOUSE FOYER

and checks his watch -- "Ten o'clock."

INT. TROPICAL PARK

"Ten o'clock." Van Pelt checks his watch. He continues to sit alone at the gazebo.

INT. HVP BUILDING - PENTHOUSE

Jake turns to the right and spots the Receptionist. A big, casual smile appears on his face. He's playing the goofy bureaucrat.

JAKE
Excuse me, ma'am, I'm Leopold Polsky, with the Attorney General's office. We know about the money laundering for Commercial First.

He hands her the warrant. While she nervously reads the official-looking document, Jake surveys the area. They appear to be alone.

JAKE (CONT'D)
We know the company is owned by Henry Van Pelt.

The Receptionist is worried, and not sure what to do. He walks past her and a small buzzer SOUNDS.

RECEPTIONIST
That's the m-metal detector, Mr. Polsky. Could you...?

JAKE
Don't worry. I'm registered. And I'll only be five minutes.

He walks right up to Van Pelt's corner office, expecting to walk in, but the door is locked.

JAKE (CONT'D)
Excuse me, ma'am, do you have a key?

The Receptionist is frantic.

RECEPTIONIST
I'm sorry, I don't. I'm really, really sorry, but....

Jake opens his briefcase and removes a small crowbar. She SQUEALS.

JAKE
Please excuse the inconvenience, ma'am.

He walks towards the door. The Receptionist is alarmed.

RECEPTIONIST
Well, let me check the lower drawer.

She "finds" the key and hands it to Jake. While Jake unlocks the office door, she surreptitiously hits a button on her phone.

VAN PELT'S OFFICE

Jake quickly lays down his custom iPad. The grid format comes up. Using the iPad, Jake walks around the office.

EXT. TROPICAL PARK - GAZEBO

Van Pelt hums a happy tune while he games on his iPhone.

INT. HVP BUILDING - VAN PELT'S OFFICE

Jake stops at the credenza and places the iPad in his pocket.

Using the crowbar, he pries the credenza open. Quickly searching, he finds the fake Eye of Ra panel. He tosses it on the floor.

Faster, he searches the credenza, then the desk. He stops momentarily and his shoulders droop in frustration.

ADRIAN (O.S.)
Where's the Eye?

Jake stands. Aims his pistol at Adrian. Then recognizes him.

ADRIAN (CONT'D)
You can put that down, Mr. Dekker. Security is on its way. I've been waiting for you.

Jake is calm.

JAKE
You can't afford to arrest me. You need me to get the panel.

ADRIAN
And you need me to get the Eye of Ra. But don't bother asking because it's not here.

Adrian moves closer to Jake.

ADRIAN (CONT'D)
And you think you will never tell us where the panel is, but you will. Eventually.

JAKE
The Eye is here. Give it to me now or I'll shoot.

But he can't. Adrian punches him in the jaw, sending him and his glasses flying over the desk and into the credenza.

Adrian grabs Jake's gun, but Jake swings the crowbar, smashing him in the head. Adrian drops to the ground unconscious.

Jake watches Adrian's head bleed. The sight sickens him, but he quickly pulls himself together, grabs the gun.

Jake glances through the office window and sees the Receptionist talking to someone on the phone.

MAIN LOBBY

The Watchman hangs up his phone. He keys something into the computer, then speaks into a walkie-talkie.

WATCHMAN
Penthouse. One intruder armed and dangerous.

VAN PELT'S OFFICE

Jake spots the Receptionist tiptoeing from the penthouse suite.

Quickly, he ransacks the office. He rips off paintings, hoping for a wall safe. Finally, the filing cabinet draws his attention. His expression says, Why didn't I try this before?

He pulls open the top drawer and finds a series of files -- all marked with the pyramid and the all-seeing eye. He looks inside the first file with an expression of amazement.

SECOND FLOOR/ELEVATOR

BROWN and STIGGINS, watch guards, step onto the elevator. Once inside, they hit "P" for penthouse. Brown places his hand over his holster.

VAN PELT'S OFFICE

Jake pulls open the second drawer, shoves his hand to the back of the cabinet drawer. He feels something. Excited, he pulls it out. It's <u>the Eye of Ra</u>, with a space for the missing panel.

Jubilantly, he plunges the tiny pyramid in his left jacket pocket. Grabs his briefcase.

PENTHOUSE

He races towards the lobby, leaping around desks and chairs.

IN THE PENTHOUSE LOBBY

The Receptionist SQUEALS in horror at the sight of Jake.

DING! -- the elevator! Like a spurred race horse, Jake gallops past the elevator to the stairway door and ducks through.

The elevator doors open. Brown and Stiggins are met by the Receptionist who points at the stairway door.

STAIRWELL

Jake takes two flights down and bursts through a door, just as Brown and Stiggins enter the stairwell two floors up.

The two watch guards race down a flight and then stop.

BROWN
Wait a minute.

They listen. They hear nothing.

BROWN (CONT'D)
Come on.

10TH FLOOR LOBBY

Jake waits for an elevator. It opens. He enters just as Brown and Stiggins burst into the lobby. The elevator door closes just in time. Brown immediately calls on his walkie-talkie.

BROWN
He's on the elevator. Hold it. It stopped on five.

MAIN LOBBY

The Watchman is into it. Checks a chart.

WATCHMAN
He's on the fifth floor. Okay, Matthew, he's yours.

MATTHEW, another guard, runs to the elevator and hits all the "up" buttons. This will force all the elevators to stop at his level. He removes his gun.

IN THE ELEVATOR

The "5" button on the control board is lit. Jake now hits "P1" for Parking First Level. The elevator door closes on the fifth floor. Down Jake goes. Fourth floor.

MAIN LOBBY

The Watchman watches the elevator. Fourth floor. Third Floor. Anticipating.

IN THE ELEVATOR

Jake watches the lights above the door. Second Floor. The elevator stops. The door opens. There, waiting for him, is Cherise Joulet, wearing a cell ear piece.

He hits the "door close" button, but Cherise stops the doors with her arm. She grabs him. He forces a smile.

JAKE
Going down?

CHERISE
Get off. They're waiting for you on the first floor.

MAIN LOBBY

Watchman anticipates as the elevator door opens. It is empty.

WATCHMAN
(smiling knowingly)
Second. He's on the second.

BASEMENT PARKING

Jake and Cherise ease through a stairway door. There are no security guards. Together, they race through the parking area and onto the street.

EXT./INT. SMART CAR

Jake and Cherise reach the car. They both jump in. He throws the briefcase into the back seat.

CHERISE
Hurry, Jake.

Jake pulls away and the two escape together.

EXT. TROPICAL PARK - CONTINUOUS

Kendall casually walks the opposite direction of the Gazebo.

Van Pelt waves his cane in the air, signaling Gray and Blue to the gazebo. He seems strangely content. He taps his ear phone.

VAN PELT
Okay, the game is on.

INT. SMART CAR - CONTINUOUS

Jake drives calmly along with Cherise as his passenger.

JAKE
I'm hoping this is another invitation to lunch because I'm starved.

She instantly produces her knife. He tenses.

CHERISE
Just hand it over and you can relax.

JAKE
I _am_ relaxed. Seems like old times.

She reaches into his coat pocket and removes his gun. He smiles at her nonchalantly.

JAKE (CONT'D)
And all along I thought you liked me.

Cherise is amused. She kisses him on the cheek.

CHERISE
... Until I saw your car.

Suddenly, he slams an elbow against her head and hits the brakes, sending her headlong into the dash.

But before he can escape, she has her knife at his throat.

CHERISE (CONT'D)
Now let me tell you why you won't try that again, Sweetheart.

She takes a couple of breaths and brushes her hair back. She is hurt, but functioning. She picks up Jake's gun.

She checks his other pocket and removes the Eye. He sighs.

CHERISE (CONT'D)
You run a troop of inner city scouts.

JAKE
Those jerk-face no-account booger eaters.

It's the worst thing Jake can think of. Cherise chuckles.

CHERISE
You have a lot of raw talent.
(MORE)

CHERISE (CONT'D)
(touches him on the cheek)
Let's keep those booger eaters safe, okay? And that tootsie you run around with, too.

Jake looks solemn. He's defeated. Cherise smiles warmly.

CHERISE (CONT'D)
Believe me, you'll fare better with me than if Adrian were here. Now drive me directly to the panel.

EXT./INT. JAKE'S HOUSE - DAY

Jake and Cherise step out of the car. Cherise takes the car keys. She leaves the briefcase in the back seat.

JAKE
You'll be destroying the lives of millions of people.

CHERISE
So? What's new?

JAKE
Personally, I favor a little peace and quiet.

CHERISE
My goal precisely.

They enter and climb the stairs.

JAKE
Your goal? I thought Van Pelt was the Grand Wizard of the New World Order.

CHERISE
Right now he is.

IN THE UPPER ROOM

The light of the afternoon sun pours through Jake's open window.

IN THE FRONT YARD

A car pulls up. Wardle, Palmer and two agents step out and draw weapons.

Mark sits in the car, looking guilty.

Wardle points to the two agents.

WARDLE
You enter the front door. Palmer, you make sure no one leaves through the front. I'll take the back.

Everyone nods. Wardle turns to Mark.

WARDLE (CONT'D)
Don't worry. No one will get hurt. You can wait in the car.

IN THE UPPER ROOM

Cherise brandishes his gun.

CHERISE
Go ahead.

Jake slow-walks past the mattress leaning against the wall, turns his head back to Cherise while sticking a hand momentarily into his pocket, and eases himself out onto the window ledge.

Cherise observes intently as he reaches up to the rain gutter.

OUTSIDE

Jake removes the real Eye of Ra panel from the rain gutter and quickly sticks a tiny piece of metal (a tracking beacon) on it.

IN THE UPPER ROOM

Jake steps back into the room with the panel.

She takes the panel. Strolls around the room, running her fingers over it. Jake is nervous -- will she find the beacon?

CHERISE (CONT'D)
Pretty smart. No one'd ever find it. Not even with a metal detector.

She stops by the doorway and inlays the panel into the Eye of Ra itself. It fits. The crystals glow. Jake looks defeated.

Cherise faces him. He stands tall, his head up. Resigned. She looks regretful.

CHERISE (CONT'D)
I'm sorry, Jake. Anyone who knows about this....

She hears the door downstairs swing open. She peers down the stairs. Two Federal Agents move quickly about.

Jake leaps to the window, dives for the rain gutter, and pulls himself out of view.

When Cherise turns around, she finds the room empty.

She smiles, glad he's gone, glad she didn't have to kill him.

CHERISE (CONT'D)
Good luck, Jake.

She dashes out the room and stealthily descends the stairs.

MAIN FLOOR NEAR THE STAIRS

An agent steps out of a room, turns, and is stabbed in the back. Cherise takes his weapon.

IN THE BACK YARD

Jake clumsily descends the vertical rain gutter, loses his grip, and drops onto the grass.

Wardle rounds the side of the house and draws a bead on Jake in the back yard.

WARDLE
Freeze!

The words are barely out of her mouth when she is nearly hit by a runaway, rusted-out Chevy clunker. The driver, Kendall Dekker.

Palmer follows on foot.

Kendall turns into the back yard and drives directly towards Jake.

Palmer aims at Kendall. Jake opens the front passenger door, gets in. Pulls Kendall's head down. Palmer's bullet misses, piercing the rear and front windshields.

JAKE
What took ya?

Jake smiles at her. She continues to drive through the back yard. He gives her a admiring look. She shrugs and confesses:

KENDALL
It was the best I could steal.

She makes a slow turn around the back of the house.

JAKE
Follow me, my wayward wife.

Before she can protest, Jake dives out and rolls into some shrubs.

WARDLE AND PALMER

watch the old clunker slow to a stop. They approach slowly, ready to fire.

AT THE RUSTED-OUT CHEVY

Palmer opens the door and no one is there.

Wardle looks back and spots Jake and Kendall sprinting into the orange grove. She turns and aims. She can't see clearly.

WARDLE
That way.

Palmer races after Jake, gun in hand. Wardle takes a slightly different route.

EXT. JAKE'S HOUSE - CONTINUOUS

Cherise steps out through the front door. No one is in the front yard. She steps into the white Smart Car and starts it.

She races past Mark sitting in Wardle's car nodding his head continuously as if praying at the Wailing Wall.

EXT. ORANGE GROVE

Jake and Kendall race through the orange grove. Palmer appears to be closing the gap.

INT. SMART CAR

Cherise drives away and pulls out her cell.

EXT. ORANGE GROVE

Jake and Kendall lurch forward, arriving at the meadow at last.

Palmer GASPS when he sees the futuristic chopper.

Wardle sees the opening ahead. She readies her pistol.

Jake inserts the crystal and the door CLICKS open. He pushes Kendall in, then jumps in over her. Just as the door CLICKS shut, Wardle arrives.

WARDLE
Holy shit, there it is!

Jake inserts the crystal into a slot in front of him. The interior lights blink on.

Palmer aims nearly point blank at the glass between him and Jake. He FIRES, but the bullets bounce off leaving no mark at all.

Jake shrugs and the Hummingbird slowly rises, the only sound a MUTED WHOP-WHOP.

Both Wardle and Palmer stare in awe.

EXT./INT. HUMMINGBIRD HELICOPTER - DAY

Jake quickly removes his custom iPad mini and tosses it to Kendall. He takes a deep breath and pulls up on the collective pitch lever.

The silence of the cockpit seems unreal. Kendall looks down at the old house and the dirt road, then at representations of the same on the iPad screen.

JAKE
I planted a beacon on the panel that's now in the Smart Car. How's that for smart?

Jake hits a spot and the blue dot appears at the top of the screen.

JAKE (CONT'D)
There she is. Fasten your seat belt.

They both do just that.

He tilts the control column and moves forward.

Following the blue dot, he searches the rural roads in his area until he spots the white Smart Car. Cherise drives towards the distant buildings of Miami.

He follows Cherise visually.

INT. SMART CAR

Cherise drives down a country road. Suddenly, the car is struck hard from above.

CHERISE
What the --

She glances out the window. She sees the helicopter.

EXT. RURAL STREETS AND AREA ABOVE - CONTINUOUS

Jake flies just above the car. There are two dents on the top of the car where the little copter struck it.

HUMMINGBIRD HELICOPTER

Jake comes down again onto the top of the car.

ON THE STREET

the car swerves.

INSIDE THE SMART CAR

The crushed roof is nearly on her head. However, Cherise regains control, her hands firmly on the wheel.

She sees an approaching overpass, lays her pistol on the passenger seat, and hits the accelerator.

HUMMINGBIRD HELICOPTER

Jake fails to notice that he's headed directly for the overpass.

KENDALL
The overpass.

A BUZZ and a red light. Jake looks forward. The overpass is in his face. He pushes the collective pitch lever.

AT STREET LEVEL

the chopper jerks up and to the left. It is headed directly for some trees. Jake has lost control.

INSIDE HUMMINGBIRD HELICOPTER

the images on the iPad screen jumble.

OUTSIDE

the bird barely clears the trees. Another overpass.

KENDALL (O.S.) (CONT'D)
Whoooooaa.

AT STREET LEVEL

the helicopter drops underneath the overpass, nearly crashing.

HUMMINGBIRD HELICOPTER

Jake has everything under control now. He is calm, but Kendall sees beads of sweat on his brow.

KENDALL (CONT'D)
We're cutting it too close.

Jake surveys the street. The white Smart Car is gone.

ON ANOTHER STREET

Cherise makes another turn.

ABOVE THE AREA

The helicopter circles like a hawk.

INSIDE THE SMART CAR

Cherise's head turns every which way, searching the unfriendly skies.

Suddenly, she sees Jake flying breakneck down the road, a yard off ground level, headed directly for the car.

OUTSIDE THE SMART CAR

Cherise hits the headlights.

HUMMINGBIRD HELICOPTER

Jake sees the car headlights blink on and off ahead, but he has turned kamikaze.

KENDALL
Oh no.

ON THE STREET

Cherise swerves onto the shoulder, the bird just missing her. The car skids out of control and caroms off a tree.

INSIDE THE SMART CAR

Cherise has blood on her face.

FROM ABOVE THE STREET

Jake's Hummingbird hovers below. The car is off the road and obscured by the trees.

INT. APACHE MILITARY HELICOPTER - CONTINUOUS

RED ROVER, a military pilot gazes in awe at the beautiful, angular, stealth Hummingbird MG-11. He speaks into his radio.

RED ROVER
This is Red Rover. I got him now.
Roger out.

EXT./INT. HUMMINGBIRD HELICOPTER

Just as Jake is about to land, he spots the Apache, then another, then another. They are everywhere. Red Rover gets Jake on the radio.

RED ROVER (V.O.)
Land your bird now and exit onto the
street, or be fired upon.

JAKE
Go ahead. Fire away.

He smiles a "Trust me" at Kendall.

INT. APACHE MILITARY HELICOPTER

Red Rover is amazed. He glances over at BLUE BOY in the next chopper. Blue Boy only shrugs: Now what?

RED ROVER
Land now and exit onto the street, or be fired upon. Final warning.

INT. HUMMINGBIRD HELICOPTER

JAKE
Wardle wants this bird too bad. You have orders not to harm it.

Jake remains silent. Confident.

His countenance falls, however, when Cherise pulls the Smart Car onto the road and drives away. He was so close.

Jake pulls up hard on the collective pitch lever.

EXT. ABOVE THE STREET

Jake's Hummingbird darts up like its namesake.

INT. APACHE MILITARY HELICOPTER

Red Rover's jaw drops.

RED ROVER
How'd he do that?

BLUE BOY (V.O.)
Where is he?

EXT. ABOVE THE STREET

In a lateral move, Jake whisks right up next to the Apache and hovers as if to draw nectar.

Red Rover stiffens in terror.

Jake aims his finger, like a gun, at Red Rover -- an angry PWHOOO!

Red Rover meekly waves. Jake flits away.

RED ROVER
Now where is he?

The Apaches hover helplessly above the area. Several of them turn their noses to the left, then right, searching for Jake.

BLUE BOY (V.O.)
Nothing on radar. What do we tell Mama Bear?

RED ROVER
He initiated cloaking device?

INT. HUMMINGBIRD HELICOPTER - MOMENTS LATER

Jake taps his custom iPad.

JAKE
Find her.

Kendall studies the screen.

EXT. OUTSIDE MIAMI - LATER

The Hummingbird glides towards Miami.

EXT. LUXURY HOTEL - LATER

Cherise drives the battered Smart Car into a nearby parking lot.

INT. HUMMINGBIRD HELICOPTER

Jake watches her run into the hotel. He notices one of many outside glass elevators ascending to the roof.

He darts over to the top of the roof and sets the copter down.

EXT. HOTEL ROOFTOP

Several couples on the observation deck observe as if this is normal.

Quickly, he steps out of his Hummingbird, tips an imaginary cap to the onlookers, and rushes to the elevator with Kendall.

INT. HOTEL LOBBY - LATER

Jake rushes to the registration desk while Kendall keeps an eye out on the lobby.

JAKE
The room of Henry Van Pelt.

ATTENDANT
I'm sorry. I'm not at liberty to share that information.

Kendall grabs Jake and points outside.

They watch Van Pelt and Cherise step into a limo.

Jake rushes across the lobby, but the limo has already turned right onto a street.

JAKE
(to Kendall)
North on Coconut Grove.

They rush to the elevator.

They force their way past some tourists and just get on.

INT. ELEVATOR

Jake acts fast. He blocks people from punching their floor number on the control panel. The door closes and the elevator begins its climb.

PASSENGER A
Hey I wanted fifth floor.

PASSENGER B
Hey jerk, hit seven.

JAKE
I'm sorry. I am in pursuit of a deadly artifact. Thank you for your cooperation.
(a courteous smile)
Please enjoy the view.

Kendall loves it. Finally, the elevator doors open.

EXT. HOTEL ROOF

Jake and Kendall bolt onto the observation deck. They stop.

The Hummingbird is gone.

Panicked, Jake searches everywhere, then notices a crowd of people, all observing something above them. Jake looks up.

Above them in the air, the Hummingbird is harnessed to, and dangles below, a huge, military chopper.

JAKE
Wardle!

INT. MILITARY CHOPPER

Wardle smiles sadistically at the tiny figure of Jake Dekker on the hotel roof.

PILOT
(into his radio)
This is Mama Bear. We're going home for porridge.

EXT. HOTEL ROOF

Jake stands helplessly looking up at his Hummingbird drifting off into the night.

He looks down at the parking lot. He spots the beat-up Smart Car, but the limo is long gone.

Kendall embraces him.

JAKE
Oh, Kenny.
(sighs)
Come on, they'll be looking for us.

EXT. SMALL AIRPORT - NIGHT

A private plane is about to taxi to the runway.

Van Pelt, Gray, Cherise (dried blood on her face) and Adrian (head heavily bandaged) step out of a small building. Gray boards first.

Van Pelt stops and embraces Adrian.

VAN PELT
The long struggle is over.

ADRIAN
Your destiny.

VAN PELT
My grand design. You will be ready?

ADRIAN
Are you kidding? I'll have ten years. Should have one helluva computer virus by then.

VAN PELT
Could be shorter.

ADRIAN
Tens years is natural. Less risk. Besides, we need ten years' technological advancement to create the ultimate unstoppable virus.

He hands a fat briefcase to Van Pelt.

ADRIAN (CONT'D)
Everything is in here. The Eye of Ra, translations as best we could figure. Coordinates, but the Eye will guide you.
(taps his iPhone)
Should have some great games in ten years, huh?

They share a brief, wistful moment.

VAN PELT
Of them all, you are the one I trust.

Adrian accepts this gratefully. Van Pelt, looking vulnerable, enjoys the acceptance.

ADRIAN
Strange. It will be just a few moments for you, but....

VAN PELT
The world will be grateful to us. Accept us. Eventually.
(laughs)
And if they don't, it will still be fun.

Adrian assists a chuckling Van Pelt into the plane.

INT. PLANE - CONTINUOUS

Van Pelt enters the cockpit with his cane and briefcase. He opens the fat briefcase. He is at once buoyant and teary. He hugs the Eye like a teddy bear. A joyful giggle escapes him.

Reverently, he places the Eye of Ra -- crystals glowing -- nearby. Hands a sheet of paper to the pilot.

VAN PELT
Fly to these coordinates.

Van Pelt sits down next to the pilot, belts himself in.

He lifts the Eye and places it on his lap.

Back in the passenger section, Gray sits across the aisle from Cherise.

Van Pelt leers at her and claps his hands lightly in delight.

Cherise looks disgusted.

EXT. SMALL AIRPORT

The plane races down the runway and takes off into the night sky.

EXT./INT. SMART CAR

Jake maneuvers down a highway in the nearly demolished car with one flat tire. The briefcase is still in the back.

Kendall watches the blue dot on the iPad screen.

EXT. ATLANTIC OCEAN - NIGHT

Van Pelt's plane flies low above the water.

INT. PLANE

Van Pelt holds the Eye in his lap. He closes his eyes.

The glowing crystals on the Eye slowly brighten.

Van Pelt continues to meditate.

The pilot's expression shows surprise, then confidence.

PILOT
I feel it.

Van Pelt just smiles like a baby in a play pen.

EXT. ATLANTIC OCEAN

The plane continues to fly low above the water. An unearthly SUCKING SOUND ends sharply with the disappearance of the plane.

INT. SMART CAR - SAME

Inside the cramped battered car, Kendall watches the iPad screen. The blue dot disappears.

Jake touches her face. They exchange expressions of despair.

INT. JAKE'S HOUSE - UPPER ROOM - NIGHT

Kendall stares through the window at the moon.

KENDALL
You sure we're safe here.

JAKE
Wardle wouldn't think I'd be stupid enough to return. Besides, I suspect she's waiting for me somewhere else.

Jake works feverishly near the drafting table. The custom iPad mini and computer are on. He stuffs papers into his pocket.

He stops and gazes at the female figure at the window. Below the window is the bed mattress with a sheet and blanket.

JAKE (CONT'D)
Kenny, we still have a shot if we can find the chopper.

She gently pulls him over to the the window. With her fingers, she gently outlines the curve of his jaw, as if he were a study in art.

KENDALL
... No matter what happens...

She curls her hands around his neck. He does not resist.

He kisses her passionately, as if doing so would stop time and erase all of their problems.

He stops, wanting to ask a painful question.

JAKE
How do I die, Kenny?

KENDALL
What are you talking about?

JAKE
You came here alone.

She drops the embrace a moment. They sit on the window sill together. She takes his hands, looks down.

KENDALL
We had to steal the Hummingbird. To get here. It didn't go as planned.
(gazing up at him)
You took a bullet meant for me.

Her chin quivers. Moonlight reflects off her watery eyes. Jake is nearly in tears himself.

KENDALL (CONT'D)
I held you in my arms. And then you....

Jake embraces her, sharing the weight of her burden.

JAKE
Oh Kenny, you've been holding all that inside?

KENDALL
And so I had to come here. I wanted to intercept that damn Eye for just one reason. To change that moment when you died.

JAKE
But the coordinates are still in the Hummingbird. If we can --

KENDALL
-- But without the Eye, the window will only take us to a moment ten years from now. You die a few days prior to that. Nothing can change your death but the Eye of Ra.

JAKE
But it's still possible to save --

KENDALL
-- I don't give a damn about the world. Screw the world! I just want to save you.

She drops her head on his shoulder. He lifts her up from the window sill and lays her carefully on the mattress.

JAKE
We'll get the chopper, sail out of here tomorrow morning and pray to God that we can get the Eye.

KENDALL
But the risks. Without the Eye, we could miss the Window. And how are we going to get the chopper?

JAKE
Kenny, we've got to try.

She nods, agreeing, loving his optimism.

KENDALL
I need you, Dream Boy.

She lays back on a pillow and gently pulls him next to her. He caresses her face, wiping away her tears and kissing them.

SERIES OF DISSOLVES - ALTERNATING PRESENT AND PAST SEAMLESSLY

-- PRESENT -- Jake kisses her behind the ear, then slides his lips down to her neck. Suddenly, he jerks his head up.

JAKE
We <u>are</u> married, right?

KENDALL
Naturally.

He returns to her neck. She lifts her face in complete surrender...

KENDALL (CONT'D)
A lot of memories ahead of you.

... And she gazes up through the window at the stars, as if making a wish.

-- FUTURE -- The stars above Sandy Beach burn brightly. LAUGHTER as Jake and Kendall swim into shore and collapse on a towel. She rolls next to him and kisses him once and then twice.

-- PRESENT -- Kendall next to Jake. She unbuttons one of his shirt buttons. He takes her arm and kisses it down to her hand.

-- FUTURE -- Jake kisses her hand. Both are in formal attire on a balcony where he takes her into his arms and dances with her slowly.

-- PRESENT -- The same slow turning of their faces; they are under a single sheet.

-- FUTURE -- They stop turning. They stand on Sandy Beach. Hand to hand, they lift their arms upward like angels, eyes riveted on each other. Then their fingers entwine.

-- PRESENT -- Fingers are entwined as the love dance concludes. Gentle, sublime. The white sheet becomes...

-- FUTURE -- ... A white sail of a sail boat. The two sail out of a beautiful bay into the open sea. Kendall lifts her face against the wind. Jake joins her. Side by side.

-- PRESENT -- They lay side by side. Then turn to each other, gaze at each other. Content. One. She brushes her hand across his jaw, and sits up. He lays back -- his eyes close, then open.

-- FUTURE -- Jake looks up, eyes glazed. Blood on his chest. Kendall cradles him. He hands her the folded yellow paper containing the coordinates. Amid tears, she calls his name.

He smiles briefly, but the smile slowly fades into death. Kendall looks up helplessly.

-- PRESENT -- Kendall looks sad, then hopeful as she gazes through the window up to the stars. We float towards them....

KENDALL (O.S.) (CONT'D)
Another time....

The sky slowly brightens and the stars disappear. It is dawn.

INT. WARDLE'S OFFICE - DAY

She works at her desk. Sips her morning brew.

A hummingbird flies up to her window. She doesn't notice. If she did, she'd see that it's not really a hummingbird....

EXT. WARDLE'S OFFICE - SAME

... It's Jake's miniature model of the Hummingbird MG-11 flitting about silently.

EXT. A STREET - CONTINUOUS

Jake works the tiny hand remote and peers into the monitor. Kendall is next to him on a Vespa scooter, some of the paneling ripped off with wires hanging loose.

In the monitor, they see Wardle through the window sipping.

INT. WARDLE'S OFFICE - CONTINUOUS

Wardle looks up at the window and the mini-chopper flits away. She has a humorous, inquisitive expression on her face -- what was that?

EXT. HOMESTEAD AIR FORCE BASE - SAME

The miniature helicopter bolts from Wardle's window and whisks around the base.

It hovers near the base laundry next to the PX (post exchange), and then darts up.

It circles over a grassy area and fenced lot where Jake's helicopter is heavily guarded. And then it flies away towards the front gate.

On her Vespa, Kendall sees the mini-chopper streak by. She drives up to the

FRONT GATE

alone. She hands the GUARD Wardle's card.

KENDALL
Bree Hawker with the Miami Herald.
Nine o'clock with J.C. Wardle.

The guard checks a clipboard.

KENDALL (CONT'D)
It's not on your docket. It's a private interview.

GUARD
Sorry, I have orders. No civilians.

Someone quickly removes the gun from the guards holster. It's Jake, who points the gun at the guard. Jake is wearing a large backpack.

Kendall pops the trunk of a nearby military vehicle...

GUARD (CONT'D)
Do I have ta?

... Jake reluctantly forces the guard inside.

In a flash, Jake enters the guard house and pushes a button. The guard gate swings up.

SOMEWHERE ON BASE

Kendall parks the Vespa.

JAKE
I still can't feel right about stealing it.

She shakes her head and removes a bag of something from Jake's backpack.

Exchanging nods, they go different directions.

The guard starts banging on the trunk.

EXT./INT. BASE LAUNDRY

Kendall steps through a back door. She spots several dry-cleaned uniforms in plastic.

A BELL RINGS and an employee goes to the counter. Jake is there.

JAKE (O.S.)
I forgot my tag.

While the employee tries to help Jake, Kendall steals a couple of Air Force "blues" uniforms.

Then she notices a nearby box marked "Lost and Found." It's filled with insignia. She grabs a handful.

CUT TO

EXT. LADIES ROOM

Kendall exits the ladies room in uniform and joins Jake, also in uniform. He notices the bird colonel insignia on her uniform.

JAKE
Hey, how come you're a colonel and I'm just a...

KENDALL
(strictly military)
... major? Complete the paper work and I'll consider it. Now carry on, maggot bait.

Jake is not sure whether to salute or not.

EXT. MILITARY VEHICLE

Two airmen open the trunk. The guard steps out.

EXT. LADIES ROOM

JAKE
Well, given our plan, I really think we should switch. Come on...

They hear a WARNING SIREN outside. She worries.

EXT. FENCED LOT

A red light flashes and a barbed wire gate shuts, sealing off the lot. Inside the lot is the Hummingbird surrounded by airmen.

EXT./INT. MILITARY BUILDING

Jake strides up to two guards in front of the building entrance. They salute him and he enters.

GUARD
Morning, Major.

Jake's return salute shows he'd rather be colonel.

The alarm continues to WAIL.

INT. WARDLE'S OFFICE

She stands at her desk, coffee mug in hand, instructing Palmer, who has his tablet and stylus.

WARDLE
Dekker's here.

JAKE (O.S.)
... And not a moment too late.

Jake throws his backpack on the desk. Wardle frantically jumps back and Palmer makes a move towards it -- is it a bomb?

JAKE (CONT'D)
Everyone relax.
(to Wardle)
You know, you really should switch to decaf.

PALMER
(deadpan)
Actually, it's herb tea. Naturally decaffeinated.

Jake nods as if impressed. Wardle quickly hits her intercom.

WARDLE
The intruder is in my office. Send security...
(an afterthought)
... And off the alarm.

Jake leans across the desk, as serious as soap.

JAKE
Before you arrest me, I want you to hear me out. Several small nuclear devices will destroy a few cities along the East Coast in about a week.

WARDLE
Cit.

Wardle studies Jake a moment, sits down. Two MPs step in.

Wardle looks at Jake. He looks back at her hopefully -- he needs her time. At last, she finally orders the MP's.

WARDLE (CONT'D)
Post outside the door. No one in or out.
(to Jake)
Okay, Dekker, let's have it.

Jake opens the backpack. He presents the files from Van Pelt's filing cabinet, each marked with the pyramid and all-seeing eye.

EXT. FENCED LOT

The red light turns off, and the barbed-wire gate opens.

Standing nearby, Kendall takes a deep breath. She approaches the guards. They salute her.

She returns the salute and steps past them carrying her bag.

GUARD
Excuse me...

Without breaking her stride.

KENDALL
Stand down, I'm inspecting the detail. Wardle's orders.

She sees the Hummingbird ahead. Her anxiety shows on her face. Marches directly to one of the airmen. The airman sees her and salutes.

KENDALL (CONT'D)
Any luck with this thing?

AIRMAN
Can't get into it. We've tried everything. Wardle requisitioned some special equipment.

KENDALL
Mind if I have a try?

The airman tries to suppress a doubtful grin, then something occurs to him.

Kendall walks up to the front door.

AIRMAN
Wait a minute, you don't have a name plate.

There is no name plate on Kendall's chest. She reaches into her bag, pulls out a remote, and pushes a big red button.

FFUSSSSH - a miniature rocket (Jake's USA X-1) shoots into the air over the base, drops its Stage-2 rocket and climbs.

This distracts the airman long enough to allow Kendall to insert the crystal pyramid key.

AIRMAN (CONT'D)
Intruder!

The helicopter door CLICKS opens, and she tosses in the bag. The Airman grabs her. She pepper sprays him.

Quickly, she hops in and shuts the door before the guards can converge on her.

The rocket reaches its zenith and explodes into a brilliant flare of light.

INT. WARDLE'S OFFICE - SAME

Wardle stares at a photocopy of a newspaper clipping about an artifact stolen in Egypt. She is thoughtful.

The brilliant light from the rocket flashes through Wardle's window. Jake -- an almost imperceptible smile.

Wardle looks wary. Palmer steps to the window.

WARDLE
So why the birdie? Why can't you go through the window in a boat?

JAKE
Because the coordinates are in the chopper.

A siren begins to WAIL again.

WARDLE
Let's see for ourselves. If they're there, I'll let you have them.
(decisively)
But the little birdie belongs to me.

EXT. WARDLE'S OFFICE - A MOMENT LATER

The entourage steps out and marches towards the lot.

Immediately, the Hummingbird descends, creating some confusion in the group.

Jake breaks into a run, racing for the chopper. Palmer pulls his gun.

INT. HUMMINGBIRD HELICOPTER

Kendall screams -- reliving a past horror.

EXT. HUMMINGBIRD HELICOPTER

Jake races toward her. Palmer draws a bead.

Wardle pulls Palmer's arm down. The gun fires harmlessly into the dirt.

Jake steps into the Hummingbird.

INT. HUMMINGBIRD HELICOPTER

JAKE
Good work, Colonel.

She wipes a tear from her eye and salutes him.

EXT. HUMMINGBIRD HELICOPTER

Wardle watches it ascend. Palmer looks confused. Wardle follows the flight of the Hummingbird.

WARDLE
If he's telling the truth, we may save our country. If he's lying, we only lose the birdie.
(lifting her gaze to meet his)
What's more important?

He looks up, and the Hummingbird flits out of sight.

EXT. ATLANTIC OCEAN - DAY

A clear, blue sky vaults over a calm, blue ocean. The only sound is the natural movement of the waves.

The Hummingbird MG-11 moves towards us at top speed.

It silently flits past and out over the ocean.

INT. HUMMINGBIRD HELICOPTER

Jake checks a large clip that holds the faded yellow paper with fold creases on it. The coordinates are circled. Shows them to Kendall, who adjusts the instruments.

He wants to say something, but hesitates; then finally:

JAKE
So uh... am I gonna be bald... you know... at the end?

KENDALL
We don't age...
(off his joyful smile)
... I think.

He frowns. The blue ocean shimmers just below them.

Almost imperceptibly the craft begins to vibrate. It vibrates more and more as it glides above the water.

Instrument readings fluctuate widely. The images on the viewing screen flutter. Then -- POP -- the computer screen BLINKS off.

KENDALL (CONT'D)
Going in.

The vibrations are very pronounced now. Jake squeezes Kendall's hand, then she places both her hands firmly on the controls.

INT. THE WINDOW IN TIME - CONTINUOUS

The blue gradually darkens to purple -- the color of the sugilite crystals. No sky. No clouds. No sea.

SOUNDS: Strange, rhythmic pulses, like thunder, only truncated at the end.

The copter seems to be motionless. Jake turns his head around. Looks up. The rotor blades move slowly and then seemingly stop.

Silence. They are in a purple void.

JAKE
Are we moving?

Straight ahead. A fold of purple-violet, like a wave, flows over the copter with a HUSHING sound, like a breeze rustling trees.

The Hummingbird gently shakes.

Another wave or fold rolls towards him -- this one stronger.

And then another, whipping the little black Hummingbird, and shaking it violently. Kendall wrestles with the control column.

Another wave, then another, with increasing frequency.

A wave twists and spirals down. The copter drops down the spiral. The violet becomes blue, yellow, red, all the colors.

The spiral twists, turns, then delivers them back into the silent, purple void.

JAKE (CONT'D)
Dang, what's that?

Straight ahead, a tiny, white dot appears. It grows bigger. It moves towards them with incredible velocity, like a bullet, but expanding.

The sound is a low RUMBLE, similar to distant thunder. Strange. Unworldly. Crescendoing...

Suddenly, the white shatters against the chopper with a sharp, deafening CLAP.

They are through the window, over the blue waters of the ocean.

EXT. ATLANTIC OCEAN - DAY - 10 YEARS IN THE FUTURE

In the distance, Miami can be seen.

Jake scans his gauges.

JAKE
Took a lot of fuel.

Kendall gives Jake a little cheer. He pulls the custom iPad mini from her bag. Flicks it on. A grid appears, then the familiar blue dot.

JAKE
They haven't returned to the past yet.

Both Kendall and Jake high-five. Jake WHOOPS it up.

They are far away from the city now, only countryside below.

JAKE (CONT'D)
Two degrees to the right. That big warehouse.

EXT. WAREHOUSE - DAY

The chopper circles the isolated warehouse. It is long -- at least 100 yards.

Near the east (right) end of the roof is a stairway that descends into the warehouse.

At the west (left) end are huge warehouse doors that are shut and a large parking lot.

The chopper ascends back over the roof and lands by the stairway. Jake jumps out of the

HUMMINGBIRD HELICOPTER

and Kendall hands him her bag and the crystal key. He helps Kendall out and shuts the helicopter door.

She strips off her uniform -- her regular clothes are underneath.

He opens the warehouse roof door, sits down on the top step and sticks his hand into the gym bag.

He removes the miniature helicopter and remote, adjusts the antenna, turns the tiny TV monitor on, and pushes a button.

The miniature helicopter whisks away. Jake peers into the tiny TV monitor, operates the control knob.

INT. WAREHOUSE

The miniature helicopter breezes through a small window near the ceiling.

The warehouse is a huge, open area with a high ceiling, like an airplane hangar. Electronics and boxes are lined on both of the long north and south walls.

At the East end, Van Pelt picks up a CD and admires it, shows it to Gray.

VAN PELT
Burn another twenty, just for insurance.

EXT. WAREHOUSE ROOF

Jake observes on his tiny monitor.

JAKE
The computer virus.

INT. WAREHOUSE

Van Pelt and Gray stroll past a futuristic luxury car with an open trunk.

The car is near a small room at the southeast corner of the warehouse. A small, high window in the room provides a view of the entire warehouse.

EXT. WAREHOUSE ROOF

JAKE'S MONITOR

shows the small room. Nearby, on a side wall, a door provides passage to a walled section that juts out -- a stairwell.

JAKE (O.S.)
Must lead to the roof.

INT. WAREHOUSE

The little Hummingbird circles up.

There is space between the small room roof and the warehouse ceiling, so the Hummingbird lands there, providing Jake with a view of the entire warehouse.

EXT. WAREHOUSE ROOF

JAKE
Everything is on the far east end...

Jake places the monitor and remote in his pocket, and stands.

JAKE (CONT'D)
... So you can take out the west.

A last solemn gaze at each other.

JAKE (CONT'D)
Are you ready?

Kendall is brave. She nods her head yes. He breaks the tension.

JAKE (CONT'D)
I'll try not to get killed this time.

She smiles momentarily in appreciation, but her eyes say she is worried.

Jake waves to Kendall, who takes off in the chopper.

EXT./INT. HUMMINGBIRD HELICOPTER

Kendall flies to the West end of the warehouse.

She hits the white button on the right dash and the missile panel CLICKS into place.

Two black panels open on either side of the chopper, and small white missiles extend outward.

She keyboards the computer and another grid appears on the passenger side of the windshield.

INT. WAREHOUSE

Jake follows the steps down

THE STAIRWELL

into the darkness.

He reaches a door, pushes it just a bit. It is open. He nods to himself, sits on a step, and peers into the TV monitor.

INT. HUMMINGBIRD HELICOPTER

Kendall locks her grid on the front doors of the warehouse.

She pushes the "Fire" button.

EXT. WAREHOUSE

One of the missiles launches -- it burns a trail to the warehouse doors and EXPLODES on impact.

INT. WAREHOUSE - SAME

The west end of the warehouse EXPLODES.

One person is hit with debris -- minor injury.

Van Pelt and Cherise step out of the small room on the east end to behold the effects of the explosion.

ON JAKE'S MONITOR

Jake can see the backs of their heads.

INT. WAREHOUSE

Everyone's eyes are westward. Then, out of the smoke, emerges the helicopter like a bird of prey.

Gray is struck with terror and falls back on his butt.

Cherise walks bravely towards it, checking her weapon. She smiles with admiration.

CHERISE
Oh, Jake.
(shouting to the others)
Dekker's here.

She gives the chopper a nod of respect as if it were Jake.

Van Pelt races towards the small room. He looks worried, then smiles wide.

VAN PELT
Oh goody! This is gonna be fun.

AT THE STAIRWELL

The door opens, and Dekker steps into the warehouse. Everyone's back is to him -- their eyes are riveted on the black bird.

IN THE WAREHOUSE EAST AREA

Gray begins firing his futuristic weapon at it to no effect.

Amid the noise, Jake glides to the car -- notes the cluttered path out the west end.

JAKE
Wouldn't hurt.

He opens the door and removes the key -- a small plastic card.

IN THE SMALL ROOM

Van Pelt places a stack of papers into the fat briefcase, then the Eye of Ra. He glances through the small, high window.

He sticks a futuristic earpiece in his ear. Taps it.

INT. BUILDING IN MIAMI

Adrian, ten years older and still bearing the scar of Jake's crowbar, nods twice to Van Pelt's voice on the other end of the line. He pockets the future version of iPhone.

Two men are with him. He speaks to the first.

ADRIAN
I need thirty men. Armed. At the warehouse now.

INT. WAREHOUSE

Gray looks up at the chopper, then sees that the west end of the warehouse is missing.

The other workers and Cherise converge on the chopper, waiting for the next move.

INT. HUMMINGBIRD HELICOPTER

Kendall begins to slowly back the chopper out. She spots Jake behind the car. He begins to crab-walk to the small room.

INT. WAREHOUSE

Jake crab-runs to the small room. He carries a gun. He sees Cherise about to turn his way. He must act or be seen.

Quickly, he opens the door and enters, his gun extended in front of him.

Cherise sees him.

IN THE SMALL ROOM

WHACK! Van Pelt's cane strikes Jake's arm. The gun drops. Van Pelt kicks it out of sight.

Jake ducks the next blow. Rolls on his back, coils, then kicks Van Pelt across the room.

BACK IN THE WAREHOUSE

Cherise races across the floor towards the small room.

IN THE SMALL ROOM

Van Pelt takes refuge behind the table, which is bare except for the fat briefcase.

Jake glances through the small window. Cherise is on her way.

Van Pelt thumps the point of his cane on the floor.

VAN PELT
Jakey-boy, have a chair. Thirty men are on their way.

He wears a happy face. Claps his hands lightly together.

VAN PELT (CONT'D)
Wanna play a game?

Jake sits and quickly produces his remote and monitor below table level.

BACK IN THE WAREHOUSE

Just as Cherise arrives at the small room door, the miniature chopper drops down near her, orbits her head once, and smacks her in the face. She backs up.

JAKE (V.O.)
I disrespectfully decline.

IN THE SMALL ROOM

VAN PELT
Oh, but we've been playing all along.
(angrily)
Look at me when I talk to you....

But Jake's head is still down; he's working his remote.

BACK IN THE WAREHOUSE

Cherise continues to back up, battling the "big bug" that continues to buzz around her.

It smacks her in the back of the head.

IN THE SMALL ROOM

Jake keeps his eye on the monitor.

VAN PELT (CONT'D)
... You should be impressed.

JAKE
Impressed? With a has-been that never was? Let's see. Rejected by your father, your girlfriend, the Congress, the world, and now me.

Jake finally looks up and is surprised to see Van Pelt nearly in tears -- stricken -- but then his pain transmutes into anger. He's about to shout something when Jake asks:

JAKE (CONT'D)
Where's the Eye?

Van Pelt glances down at his briefcase lying on the table between Jake and himself. His mistake registers on his face.

Jake puts his feet up against the table and instantly shoves it hard into Van Pelt's mid-section, pinning him against the wall.

The wind knocked out of him, Van Pelt collapses onto the floor. His cane rolls under the table. If he had any air in his lungs, he'd moan in pain.

Jake tries to manage the remote....

BACK IN THE WAREHOUSE

... But Cherise finally swats the mini-copter out of the air and stomps on it. It does little damage except to bend the rotors, so it can no longer fly.

Her hand bleeding, she purposefully eyes the small room.

IN THE SMALL ROOM

Jake takes the briefcase and opens it. Inside is the Eye of Ra. He CLICKS the case shut and sits it beside the door.

Van Pelt tries to catch his breath, sees Jake by the door.

BACK IN THE WAREHOUSE

Cherise approaches the room, her gun ready.

IN THE SMALL ROOM

Jake waits. Van Pelt smiles his cheery smile -- he's not worried. Jake looks nervous.

The door opens.

VAN PELT
Cherise, watch out.

His warning actually diverts her attention.

Jake grabs her gun hand and swings her hard across the room. The gun FIRES harmlessly into the wall.

Van Pelt scurries under the table and grabs his cane.

Jake wrenches the gun from her hand.

His victory is ever so brief as Van Pelt's cane comes down on his head. Jake crumples to the ground.

The gun drops to the floor and Jake lies dazed but conscious.

Cherise glances at the expectant Van Pelt, then seizes the opportunity to grab the briefcase and is out the door before Jake can grab the gun.

Van Pelt is mortified.

BACK IN THE WAREHOUSE

Cherise flees through the door of the small room carrying the briefcase.

IN THE SMALL ROOM

Van Pelt tries to help himself up. He is in a panic.

VAN PELT
The Eye!

Jake takes advantage of the diversion. Yanks the cane from Van Pelt. Delivers a blow to the ribs. Scoops up Cherise's gun. Stumbles to the door.

BACK IN THE WAREHOUSE

Cherise races to the car. But the car key is gone.

She scans the area. Spots the chopper gliding out of the warehouse and up.

Jake strides out into the warehouse area, spots Cherise, produces his gun; but she darts through the warehouse stairway door before he can shoot.

IN THE STAIRWELL

Jake climbs the stairs as quietly as possible. He's alert, expecting Cherise at any minute.

One flight. Then two. Three. Nothing.

He reaches the top.

EXT. WAREHOUSE ROOF

Jake bursts through the door and ducks, makes a clumsy roll, then stands up and points his gun.

Cherise is waiting for him. Jake points the gun at her.

He is at the east end. A few yards to his right is the chopper. Kendall steps out cautiously.

About 20 yards in front of him is Cherise and the long, flat roof behind her, a large portion of the west end missing.

CHERISE
Seems like old times.

JAKE
Drop the briefcase and get out of here now.

She stops and smiles mysteriously. Then keeps coming. Slow. Calm. Smiling warmly.

Kendall spots several vehicles approaching the jagged west end.

KENDALL
Jake, they're coming.

CHERISE
And they're not here for a picnic.

Cherise steps forward, the briefcase in her left hand. Jake is a rock. But will he crumble?

JAKE
They'll skin you alive when they learn you double-crossed Van Pelt.

Cherise wilts. She glances back.

AT THE WEST END OF THE ROOF

Adrian and his men climb the jagged and crumbling west side of the warehouse. He rubs his scar.

ON THE EAST END OF THE ROOF

CHERISE
You can have the Eye, but you get me, too.
(a sexy wink)
Otherwise, you'll have to kill me. And I don't think you want to do that.

Cherise steps up to Jake. Her face softens. She gazes at Jake tenderly.

JAKE
Believe me. I care enough about her to shoot you.
(extends the car key with his left hand)
You can escape back down the stairs. Or die. Now drop the briefcase.

Meanwhile, some of Adrian's "soldiers" have reached the rooftop.

Cherise looks resigned and calm.

CHERISE
Okay, Sweetheart, but I'll miss you.

With her left hand, she extends the briefcase towards Jake's firing hand.

IN SLOW MOTION

-- The knife flicks into Cherise's right hand.

-- Jake's eyes show he expected this. He jerks his arm into firing position.

-- Cherise swings the knife towards his neck.

-- The gun EXPLODES like a cannon shot.

-- Jake jerks his head back. The knife misses its mark.

-- Cherise's expression shows shock and surprise as she falls backwards with a stomach wound.

-- The briefcase flies twenty yards towards Adrian's men.

-- Kendall looks shaken.

IN REAL TIME

Jake gazes at his fallen foe -- horrified, yet relieved.

She looks at Jake -- shocked, helpless.

Kendall is nearly in tears. She runs to him.

Jake looks at the briefcase twenty yards away, then at the men racing towards him. Some kneel and prepare to fire. He's torn -- it's either Kendall or the briefcase.

KENDALL
Get the briefcase!

JAKE
The chopper.

She starts towards the briefcase, but Jake embraces her.

KENDALL
But the Eye of Ra.

Quickly, he carries her to his Hummingbird. He inserts the crystal into the door lock. The door CLICKS open and Kendall, then Jake, jump in.

AT THE HUMMINGBIRD HELICOPTER

As the door shuts, dozens of bullets ricochet off the chopper.

Jake frantically inserts the crystal into the ignition slot.

JAKE
I'm sorry, it was either you or the Eye.

KENDALL
We can still....

Jake nods. Hits a control.

ON THE WAREHOUSE ROOF

Cherise, weak and bleeding, tries to crawl to the briefcase.

Van Pelt emerges through the nearby warehouse roof door.

The Hummingbird leaps over Cherise and scoots over to the briefcase, touching down. Jake opens his door.

EXT./INT. HUMMINGBIRD HELICOPTER

At the same time, Adrian climbs over the top of the chopper, careful to stay below the rotors.

He begins to aim at the back of Jake's head as Jake leans out the door to grab the briefcase.

Kendall spots Adrian.

KENDALL
Jake. Above.

But Jake doesn't hear her. He catches the briefcase handle.

Kendall grabs him and jerks him back in. The briefcase falls to the ground.

At that same moment, Adrian fires, missing Jake. Adrian tumbles off the chopper onto the briefcase.

Adrian gets on one knee. Kendall dives across Jake, pulls the door shut as Adrian fires.

And then its a hail storm of bullets as soldiers surround the chopper. Bullets ricochet off the Hummingbird.

Kendall eases back into her seat, a faint smile on her face. She reaches for Jake's face. Jake breathes a sigh of relief.

JAKE
That was a close call.

And then he sees the blood.

JAKE (CONT'D)
Oh Kenny no. Kenny. Kenny.

He holds her delicately. His face shows agony.

KENDALL
He was going to shoot you.

EXT. WAREHOUSE ROOF

Adrian grabs the briefcase just as Van Pelt arrives.

Jake's helicopter pulls up slowly.

The Hummingbird wobbles as men fall from the chopper like ants. One catches the silent rotor blades and is sliced in two.

Cherise glances up at Jake with a betrayed look.

CHERISE
Farewell, Jake.

INT. HUMMINGBIRD HELICOPTER

Jake watches helplessly as the men grab Cherise. They hold her up in standing position while Van Pelt impales her with her own knife.

Van Pelt then opens the briefcase to find the Eye of Ra.

KENDALL
We have to destroy it. It's too dangerous in his hands. Besides, it hardly matters now.

She shows him the blood on her.

EXT. ABOVE THE WAREHOUSE ROOF

The Hummingbird darts away, flies out over the ocean, then turns around and faces the warehouse.

Kendall sits up, brings up the grid and locks on the group of people on the roof.

KENDALL
Melt it down.

She fires the second and last missile.

The missile burns through the air and strikes the warehouse roof.

The men, Van Pelt, Adrian, the Eye of Ra, the beautiful Cherise... disintegrate.

And all sound dissipates into an eerie silence.

Jake closes his eyes, then opens them. The flames billow up.

Kendall squeezes Jake's hand.

KENDALL (CONT'D)
To Sandy Beach.

But Jake frantically moves the Hummingbird inland (westward).

JAKE
You need a doctor.

Kendall shakes her head.

KENDALL
I'm dying. Besides, how do you explain
the warehouse? And this Hummingbird
is stolen property.
Take me to Sandy Beach! Jake.

She puts her hand on his arm. Her face is calm, composed.

EXT. SANDY BEACH - LATER

Kendall lays in Jake's arms on a grassy area near the beach. Behind them is the Hummingbird.

KENDALL
Sandy Beach holds many memories for
us. You'll find out. So this is where
you'll leave me. In my own time.

JAKE
Are you in pain?

KENDALL
Not now. Just my life bleeding out.
I'm happy. Because...

He looks at her quizzically. Her expression is hopeful and serene.

KENDALL (CONT'D)
... now I'm going to pass through
another window. And I believe you'll
be there... on the other side waiting
for me... where sorrow becomes joy.

She strokes his jaw.

KENDALL (CONT'D)
... Just like I'm waiting -- the younger
me -- waiting for you through there.

She points out to sea, to the "Window." Jake tries to stifle a sob. Kendall responds with dry humor.

KENDALL (CONT'D)
The only couple in history to both
live and die for each other.
Where's Oprah when you need her?

Jake embraces her gently.

KENDALL (CONT'D)
Some people live a lifetime without love. We have ten years, Dream Boy.

JAKE
I love you, Kendall. And will.

KENDALL
Now make me a promise, Jake. When we meet...

JAKE
... On Saturday...

KENDALL
... on Saturday, don't tell me anything about the future. Nothing.
We live and love in the present.
Promise me.

JAKE
I promise.

KENDALL
(in Jake's voice)
And when Jake Dekker makes a promise...

Kendall coughs, smiles, and breathes a long sigh. She's fading.

KENDALL (CONT'D)
And be my obedient boy scout.

They smile at each other.

JAKE
But how do I meet you? Where --

Her body falls limp.

Jake holds her and weeps.

And the ocean waves roll in and roll out.

MOMENTS LATER

We accelerate out to sea, just above the waves, moving faster and faster. Out to the blue Atlantic.

INT. HUMMINGBIRD HELICOPTER - DAY

Jake continues flying over the blue Atlantic.

Sadly, he checks his coordinates on the faded yellow paper.

Fuel indicator is on empty. The black bird begins to vibrate.

The sky changes hue to purple. Then: The strange, rhythmic pulses of sound, like thunder, only truncated in the end.

EXT. THE OCEAN - SAME

The Hummingbird disappears into the window. There is only blue sky.

EXT. BERMUDA TRIANGLE - DAY - PRESENT DAY

Blue sky. An unwordly, deafening CLAP...

... And then silence.

The Black Hummingbird suddenly appears. Its movements are erratic. And it plunges into the sea.

ON THE SURFACE

Jake pops up. He GASPS for air.

LATER

A very tired Jake Dekker bobs on the water, still treading.

He spots a sailboat. He shouts for help.

LATER

The sailboat glides alongside him.

EXT. SAIL BOAT - CONTINUOUS

A hand reaches down to pull him up.

He helps himself on, rolls on his back, and looks up into the face of KENDALL -- 10 years younger.

When he sees who she is, he jumps up, then nearly falls -- a little dizzy from all that time at sea.

He gazes at her in wonder as if emerging from a dream. Chin quivers. He almost says her name, almost embraces her, but catches himself.

Kendall is caught in his gaze momentarily, then chuckles.

KENDALL
How long you been out there, sailor?
(assessing him)
Kinda sunstroke and water-logged.

She chuckles again, then Jake blurts out:

JAKE
Is it Saturday?

KENDALL
(nods "yes")
Maybe you better lie down.

Jake looks content until Mark strides up.

MARK
What did you reel in, Kendall?

Mark suddenly stops -- is that Jake?

Kendall makes introductions.

KENDALL
(to Jake)
Oh, this is Mark. I'm Kendall.
And you are...

Jake is too stunned to talk. Closes his eyes.

She waves her hand in front of his face, trying to wake him out of his dream-like trance.

KENDALL (CONT'D)
Ahhh, Dream Boy....

No reaction. She shrugs to Mark

KENDALL (CONT'D)
This is Dream Boy.

She looks pleased with the nickname.

JAKE
Dream Boy?

Mark is amused. Jake shakes his head -- recovering -- then escorts Mark a few feet from Kendall. Mark looks scared.

MARK
You're not mad at me are ya, I hope,
for telling them where your secret
hideout was. I --

JAKE
-- Mark, all is forgiven...
(whispering)
... but Kendall...

Mark slugs him in the arm.

MARK
... I was gonna set ya up anyway. I
told ya.

And that he did, back in the second scene. Both Mark and Jake are happy with the deal. They shake. Reconciled.

KENDALL
Sun's about to go down. Let's head to Sandy Beach.

Jake winces when he hears "Sandy Beach."

KENDALL (CONT'D)
Have you ever been there?

Jake keeps his promise and lies.

JAKE
No.

EXT. THE OCEAN

The sail boat turns towards the shore and pushes away. The happy voices of Kendall and Jake become faint.

Soon Kendall pushes Jake back into the ocean. He crawls back onto the boat amid laughter.

And they sail to home shore and into the sunset.

EXT. COAST GUARD CUTTER - DAY

Jake's Hummingbird MG-11 is hoisted from the ocean by the cutter's crane.

Wardle, "herb tea" coffee cup in hand, watches from the deck while Palmer stands with his tablet and stylus.

WARDLE
Get Dekker in. Monday. Tell him he's working for me now...
(a sip of herb tea)
... making little birdies.

FADE TO BLACK.

POSSIBLE SEQUEL

DREAM GIRL or DREAM BOY is the story of how Jake dies in Kendall's arms ten years later, and how she escapes (to present time) in his Hummingbird with the help of his inner-city scouts (now teens and young adults).

In a way, it would be more of PREQUEL than a SEQUEL. This creates a perfect circle in time: A WINDOW IN TIME (alternate title: DREAM BOY) is how Kendall dies for Jake, and DREAM GIRL is how Jake dies for Kendall. And both are how the two live for each other.

A SUMMER WITH HEMINGWAY'S TWIN

by Dave Trottier & Lucille S. deView

~ adapted from the stage play of the same title ~

HISTORY & CONTENT

Lucille S. deView, newspaper writing coach as well as my client and student, contacted me one day with the exciting news that her play had won the National Play Award. She wondered if I would write a screenplay based on the play.

I read the play and told her I would be honored, although I didn't get started until much later. I also told her I would like her to have a screenwriting credit since she would be offering comments on my various drafts, making sure I was true to the time (1939) and the real-life characters.

The biggest writing challenges were strengthening conflicts, dramatizing events, and transforming a dialogue-heavy stage play into a filmic story with visual elements and scenes. I even alluded to a few incidents from Ernest Hemingway's life, such as the plane crash and his father's suicide.

This was to be a literary or lyrical screenplay that writers, Hemingway fans, and others could enjoy. Clients and students may get a kick out of a couple of short poems in the script. That's because I've stated in class and script evaluations that poetry is generally not for movies. You can decide whether or not they work in this script.

When I began the marketing phase in 2005, I was surprised at how many people missed the implications of certain characters being "twins" of some kind, so I made those instances a bit more obvious in the script by using the term "twin" or by underscoring.

There are actually five sets of "twins" in this screenplay. See if you can catch them: Marcelline and Ernest Hemingway (thus, the title), Willis and Ernest, Marcelline and Lila, Lila and Willis, and Thomas and Ernest.

The whippoorwill represents Lila's writing voice, and since Lila "worships" Ernest, there are plenty of religious symbols. The lantern is Ernest's literary light. And you will see what the deer is.

As you know, music is not the writer's department. Even so, I made use of the viola since that's what Marcelline played in real life. I mention one song (an aria) in the script, "One Fine Day," that I believe is in the public domain. I selected it because it's from an opera that Ernest and Marcelline watched together when they were young.

* * *

The marketing process was slow, but positive. Many companies expressed interest, including Sally Field's company which almost bought it. On the Bus Productions, which had a deal with 20th Century Fox, made a very generous option offer, and they renewed the option twice. In addition, I contributed as an associate producer.

Two fine actresses expressed interest in the project: Anne Hathaway (who later won an Academy award) to play Lila, and Mariel Hemingway (Oscar-nominated actress, who was about the same age as Marcelline at the time) to play Marcelline.

Fully committed and ready to start were the following: Alfonso Arau (Golden Globe-nominated director of *Like Water for Chocolate* and *A Walk in the Clouds*), Eugenio Zanetti (Academy Award-winning art director), and Vittorio Storaro (three-time Academy Award-winning cinematographer). I was very happy with these additions. We also had a casting director and a production manager familiar with Michigan locations. The Michigan Film Office was licking their chops for our eventual arrival.

Finally, an offer was made to Judi Dench to play the role of Mrs. Hemingway (Ernest's mother). If Ms. Dench accepted, the script would be produced. She considered it, but ultimately declined. This greatly discouraged the production company and they suddenly dropped the project. They later expressed regret for doing this.

WHY PUBLISH THE SCRIPT?

One reason for publishing this script is it may be the closest I'll come to getting it out there for people to enjoy. There are two other more important reasons.

This book will be purchased primarily by writers and *A Summer with Hemingway's Twin* is about writers and writing.

In addition, it's a successful spec script in correct format, something great numbers of clients and students have requested.

ABOUT THE FORMAT

The script is in correct, industry standard, spec screenplay format. There could be a few minor errors I missed. I avoided camera directions and used very few editing directions. The script appears in 10-point Courier New (rather than the standard 12-point font) to fit the dimensions of this book, but it looks like a script should look. The tabs are correct.

Because of the script's somewhat arty style and period (mostly 1939), the narrative description and dialogue are not quite as lean as in *A Window in Time* and the pacing not quite as fast, but the story and character development run deeper.

I sincerely hope you find the script both readable and enjoyable. If you have a question or comment about the writing or format, please contact me at dave@keepwriting.com.

PHOTOS

The following photos were provided by Lucille deView and the Kennedy Library in Boston. These were not included with the script during the marketing process.

Ernest as a boy

Marcelline

Marcelline snapped this photo of Ernest as a teen in front of his tent holding the woodchuck he had shot

Ernest after World War I

The front of Marcelline's cabin on Walloon Lake, Michigan. The screened porch is on your left as you face the cabin; it's somewhat obscured by darkness.

A SUMMER WITH HEMINGWAY'S TWIN

by Dave Trottier & Lucille S. deView

adapted from the stage play of the same title

Dave Trottier
4456 Manchester St.
Cedar Hills, UT 84062
801/492-7898
dave@keepwriting.com

FADE IN (IN SEPIA TONE):

A black metal scales for weighing food for diabetics.

INT. MRS. HEMINGWAY'S KITCHEN - SAME

GRACE HALL HEMINGWAY, wearing a Victorian gown, washes apples while singing the aria "One Fine Day." She's practicing. A music stand with sheet music is nearby.

SUPER: "December 6, 1928"

She hears a door open and stops momentarily. DR. HEMINGWAY, 57, full beard, limps into the kitchen looking careworn.

Mrs. Hemingway notices the limp and looks alarmed. He kisses her affectionately on the cheek. She gestures to the scales.

MRS. HEMINGWAY
If you'd stay on your diet....

His expression turns dark when he sees the diabetic scales.

MRS. HEMINGWAY (CONT'D)
Marcelline's pregnant.

Dr. Hemingway allows himself a weak smile.

He climbs the stairs, clinging to the banister, then stops and gazes mournfully at his upbeat wife -- a farewell look. His hand removes a gun from his pocket.

Mrs. Hemingway slices apples joyfully and resumes singing.

She places a cup of apple slices on the scale, carefully weighing them. She removes a slice -- just right.

Suddenly, a GUNSHOT EXPLODES from upstairs.

(Note: what follows is in color, except where indicated.)

INT. COTTAGE - DAY

The anguished face of MARCELLINE HEMINGWAY SANFORD, 41, reacts to the memory of that loud GUNSHOT.

She sits at a desk where she has been typing. She sniffs quietly and touches her head -- a headache. A 1939 calendar is pinned to the wall.

Her hand returns the portable typewriter carriage. SLAM!

INT. BUS - DAY

SLAM! -- The bus doors shut. LILA, 21, wears a frayed sweater over her rumpled dress, boys' black gym shoes, and her ever-present floppy, red hat -- a refugee from the inner city. She hurries to a seat and looks out the window. No one there.

EXT. DETROIT BUS STATION - CONTINUOUS

The old bus lumbers out of the filthy station.

INT. BUS (MOVING)

Lila gazes at aging factory buildings and dismal streets.

She hugs a Hemingway novel to her chest, lays her head back, smiles, and closes her eyes.

BLACKNESS

The roar of the bus and city sounds FADE to silence.

Then... the call of a lone whipporwill summons our attention.

FADE IN:

The whipporwill on a pine bough suddenly takes flight. She flies into the silvery light of a mid-June dawn.

FIRST SUPER: "All references to Ernest Hemingway and his relatives are historical."

SECOND SUPER: "The Hemingway women are depicted as they were in 1939."

EXT. WALLOON LAKE - DAY

Loons cry and yodel as they swoop over forests and a secluded inland lake where fingers of morning mist rise from the water.

THIRD SUPER: "Walloon Lake, Michigan, 1939."

Near the water's edge, shrouded in the mist, lies a doe amid ferns. She stands -- harmless, wise, mystical -- then darts into the dark wood.

Our whippoorwill dips past, leads us to a boarded-up, long-deserted white cottage overgrown with vines -- Windemere -- a ghost of Hemingway's boyhood.

She soars again toward the shore of a nearby brown-stained cottage. This one is occupied.

A plaintive melody played on a viola drifts from the window into the open air.

SEPIA FLASHBACK - THE WALLOON SHORE

CHILD ERNEST HEMINGWAY, age 5, wears an overlarge straw hat and carries a fishing pole over his shoulder like a proud soldier carrying a rifle. He stops. Notices something. His smile widens in anticipation. Drops his pole.

CHILD MARCELLINE (Ernest's "twin"), 6, runs to him.

CHILD MARCELLINE
Ernie, Ernie, what did you catch?

Child Ernest retrieves two small bass from a woven basket slung over his shoulder with a strap.

CHILD ERNEST
Look, Mazaween.

The viola solo stops.

INT. COTTAGE - CONTINUOUS

Marcelline Hemingway is lost in her memory -- her left hand curled around the viola neck, the bow in her right.

EXT. COTTAGE - DAY

Marcelline strolls from the cottage in a long wool robe over a flannel nightgown and moccasins, hugging herself against the chill. She puts a hand to her head, nursing a headache.

Approaching the shore, she pauses to inhale the scent of pines and damp, musky earth. Her smile is blissful again -- the headache forgotten as she communes with the wild.

She scans the sky as the loons fly in. As they glide onto the calm lake, she smiles her "I'm home again" smile.

Suddenly inspired with a thought, she silently rushes into a screened porch that's part of the cottage.

INT. COTTAGE - MOMENTS LATER

Marcelline sits at her small desk amid mismatched furniture, family photos, books, art, and a Victrola.

On the desk is a portable typewriter, the one she's been using. She rolls a sheet of paper into it, then glances at a stack of manuscripts. She turns her ear to the sound of the whippoorwill calling outside.

EXT. COTTAGE - PINE TREE

On a pine bough, the lone whippoorwill stutters: "Whip-whip-whip, whip-poor, whip-poor, whip-poor."

The bird flutters away as a hand lifts a pail from a nail on the tree.

The hand belongs to Lila, wearing the same frayed sweater, black gym shoes, and red felt hat she wore on the bus.

At the nearby hand pump, she pumps water into the pail and splashes it onto her face, drying herself with a towel. Then she empties the pail and pumps it full of fresh water.

She gazes at the pewter sky. Soon she hears the whippoorwill, who has returned to her pine bough.

Lila smiles at the bird, who again stutters: "Whip-whip-whip, whip-poor, whip-poor, whip-poor."

LILA

Easy there little bird. You can do it. Easy now.

The whippoorwill sings her entire song: "Whippoorwill, whippoorwill, whippoorwill."

LILA (CONT'D)

There, see? It wasn't so hard to get your song right, was it?

Lila laughs, picks up the pail and heads across the back yard to the cottage screened porch. The sound of typing alarms her and she hurries inside.

INT. COTTAGE

Marcelline looks up from typing at the squeak of the screen door.

MARCELLINE

Don't slam...

The door slams.

MARCELLINE (CONT'D)

... Ah, well.

LILA

Oh, no, Mrs. Sanford. Did I oversleep?

MARCELLINE

No, no. One of my blinding headaches woke me.

LILA

I'm glad. I mean, I'm glad I'm not late.

Lila puts the pail in the kitchen, returns, and starts setting the table for breakfast as Marcelline types, then pauses.

MARCELLINE
Besides, it's my favorite time of the day.

LILA
The loons startled me this morning, yodeling and laughing like maniacs.

MARCELLINE
I told you, Walloon Lake is enchanted.

LILA
With stuttering whippoorwills, and fireflies at night.

Lila surreptitiously peers at what Marcelline is typing.

LILA (CONT'D)
My American Lit class'd die. Imagine being where Ernest summered as a boy. Imagine walking on holy ground.

MARCELLINE
It's hardly holy.

LILA
And working for his sister.

Marcelline slaps the typewriter carriage across.

MARCELLINE
Oh? That's who I am? Ernie's sister?

LILA
I didn't mean --

Lila bites her nails.

MARCELLINE
-- I have another brother, Leicester. And three sisters. But it's always Ernie.

LILA
No, truly. When I saw your ad at college signed Marcelline Hemingway ... uh... Sanford, well, I was delirious.

MARCELLINE
(teasing)
You won't be delirious when you do the laundry by hand. Freshen my coffee, Lila, and bring me an aspirin. And don't slam...

As Lila hurries to the kitchen, the Dutch-door slams behind her.

MARCELLINE (CONT'D)
... the door.

IN THE KITCHEN

Lila pours coffee from a percolator and scoops a tiny aspirin tin from a drawer. The kitchen is small.

LILA
My brother Thomas has never seen the woods....

Marcelline sticks her head in. Lila follows her onto the

SCREENED PORCH

where she sets the coffee cup beside Marcelline, then pops open the aspirin tin for her.

MARCELLINE
Hope you won't get lonesome, Lila. The girl last summer missed her friends. I had to send her home.

She chases her aspirin with a sip of coffee and leafs through notes. Lila dusts.

LILA
I won't. I have my writing. That's enough.

MARCELLINE
Is it? I think about the Old Brute, and I wonder.

LILA
Will the Old Brute -- I mean, will your brother visit this summer?

MARCELLINE
What would you do if he did?

LILA
I'd show him my stories and poems. Ask him: Why does this work? Why not that?

As Lila dusts framed photos, one photo catches her attention.

She looks carefully at the photograph of TEENAGED ERNEST holding a dead woodchuck and standing in front of his tent.

MARCELLINE
Well, don't count on him. He never comes to Walloon.

LILA
Mrs. Sanford. Is that Ernest?

Marcelline turns and peers at the photo.

MARCELLINE
Yes, that's Ernie. He moved into his tent when our little sisters arrived.

LILA
Did he write in his tent?

MARCELLINE
Yes, by lantern light. He set deadlines, even then. So I set one, too. Write one scene a week, and finish my play by summer's end.

LILA
What's your play about, Mrs. Sanford?

MARCELLINE
About growing up with my doctor-daddy and my artist mother. And...
(for Lila's benefit)
... the Old Brute.

Marcelline stands, leads Lila outside.

EXT. WALLOON LAKE - DAY

The two walk along the pristine shore. Marcelline uses a walking stick.

LILA
It must've been exciting to grow up as Ernest's twin.

MARCELLINE
Hardly twins. I was eighteen months older.

LILA
But my professor said you were dressed alike -- had the same crib, same toys, and...

MARCELLINE
... same ambition to write.
(MORE)

MARCELLINE (CONT'D)
(setting the record straight)
Mind you, raising us as twins was one of mother's more dramatic notions.

LILA
My professor said that Ernest showed you his first published poems before anyone else.

Marcelline halts and looks wistfully into the trees.

MARCELLINE
We were great pals. Saw Madam Butterfly when we were in our teens. We cried at the end....

LILA
Imagine!

MARCELLINE
... But that was a long time ago. Before --

A gunshot EXPLODES, reverberates. Marcelline winces -- the flash of a painful memory.

MARCELLINE (CONT'D)
Probably a poacher. I can't bear that sound.

Marcelline squares her shoulders, picks up her walking stick, and forges ahead. Lila follows as they approach a stream.

MARCELLINE (CONT'D)
Hope you're not afraid of snakes, like the girl last year. Silly girl.

Lila looks down, steps warily.

LILA
Silly to be scared of... snakes.

They cross the stream on rocks and find the watercress. Lila almost falls in picking it.

MARCELLINE
The watercress is for a tea I'm giving Mother tomorrow. Gather plenty.

LILA
She's coming here? Ernest's mother? God.

Lila catches her reference to "Ernest's mother." She smiles a sickly, deferential smile. Bites her nails.

MARCELLINE
And while she's here, don't wear your hat in the house.

Lila whips off her hat, even though they are outdoors.

MARCELLINE (CONT'D)
And don't say God.

Marcelline studies her momentarily.

MARCELLINE (CONT'D)
You should cut your hair in a Page Boy. Tidy up your clothes. If you don't spruce up, you'll never catch a beau.

LILA
Don't wanna catch a beau. I see girls who hang out at dance halls, an' flirt, an' have babies, an' never amount to anything.

MARCELLINE
But dancing's fun. Even bobbed my hair and did the Charleston. Fancy that.

Marcelline, suddenly giddy, does a few dance steps and laughs.

Suddenly she grimaces in pain, totters. Lila catches her. She steadies.

MARCELLINE (CONT'D)
Mercy. I can't be sick. Not now. My writing. And the more I want things to go smoothly when Mother visits....

LILA
Don't worry. I'll have things shipshape before she gets here.

MARCELLINE
(recovering)
Have to put the Charleston in my play. Think your American Lit class'd like to see a play about the Hemingways?

LILA
Oh, imagine what we'd learn about Ernest as a boy. I mean, about all of you.

MARCELLINE
(with wry resignation)
You mean about Ernest.

Lila points to ferns pressed down, as if for a bed. She's serious. It's a mystical moment.

LILA
Has someone been sleeping here?

MARCELLINE
Hoofprints. See? Probably a deer.

Lila spots something -- a tuft of fur. She has an expression of wonder.

Marcelline plucks the fur from the ferns and gives it to a wide-eyed Lila.

MARCELLINE (CONT'D)
We see fewer deer these days.

Lila steps into the dark wood. Marcelline escorts her. They scuff through dry leaves and step over logs, then enter a clearing. Lila holds her hat to her heart.

LILA
Ernest's woods. His cathedral. I dreamed of seeing his hemlock tree struck by lightning, his oaks, his --

MARCELLINE
-- Hushhhhhh.
(whispers)
Close your eyes. Listen. Don't move.

Lila obeys. They stand in silent

BLACKNESS

A bird twitters. A crow caws. A branch creaks. The wind ruffles the leaves.

SEPIA FLASHBACK - EXACT SAME CLEARING

Teenaged Ernest strides into the clearing. He holds a dead woodchuck in his left hand, while a shotgun is "bent" over his right forearm. He carries it like the arm of a fine lady.

TEENAGED MARCELLINE snaps a photograph of him in front of the tent, the one we saw earlier.

Ernest throws the woodchuck her way and she screams. Then they both laugh.

TEENAGED ERNEST
Come here, I want you to read something.

He ducks into his tent, followed by Marcelline. He hands her a few pages. His lantern is nearby.

TEENAGED ERNEST (CONT'D)
No one's seen them. What do you think? No mercy, now.

A breeze catches the tent flap, which closes, cutting off the light.

BLACKNESS

A BLAST of Glen Miller music.

FADE IN:

INT. COTTAGE - DAY

Marcelline opens her eyes. She's at her desk typing furiously.

MARCELLINE
Carol, turn that down.

The music drops several decibels, obviously coming from a nearby bedroom. Marcelline types away, notices some nearby letters.

SCREENED PORCH

Lila, wearing her felt hat, ponders the photo of Ernest holding a dead woodchuck by his tent.

MARCELLINE (CONT'D)
Lila!

MARCELLINE'S DESK AREA

Lila approaches Marcelline, still typing.

MARCELLINE (CONT'D)
Put these letters to Sterling -- to Mr. Sanford -- in the mailbox.

She stops typing. Sighs.

MARCELLINE (CONT'D)
Wish he didn't have to work in the city.

Marcelline hands Lila a manila envelope.

MARCELLINE (CONT'D)
And put this in the mailbox, too.
(with some pride)
It's my play about club women, the one Samuel French published.

LILA
Samuel French?

MARCELLINE
A women's group in Minnesota's producing it.

LILA
On the stage? Your play?

MARCELLINE
On the stage. My play.

LILA AND MARCELLINE
Imagine.

Lila darts for the door with the letters and manila envelope.

EXT. COTTAGE - CONTINUOUS

Mrs. Hemingway -- liberated, yet wearing a Victorian gown and picture hat -- carries a painting.

Lila busts through the screen door like a bat, scaring the daylights out of the 64-year-old dame. The letters and manila envelope fly everywhere.

LILA
M-m-m-missus Hemingway?
(removes her hat)
We didn't expect you today. Mrs. Sanford -- er -- she's typing.

MRS. HEMINGWAY
Poor Marcelline. She pushes too hard. I pray for her.

Lila gathers the letters. Mrs. Hemingway looks around wistfully and hands her painting to Lila, who drops the letters again to hold the painting.

MRS. HEMINGWAY (CONT'D)
Bring me a dipper of water, please. I love to drink from the dipper.

IN THE BACK YARD

Lila props the painting on the work table and fills a dipper from the squeaky pump. She offers it to Mrs. Hemingway, now settled in a lawn chair.

MRS. HEMINGWAY (CONT'D)
You must be the girl who wants to write like Ernie.

LILA
Yes, ma'am.

MRS. HEMINGWAY
I don't understand why. The things he writes these days.... But he was a precious boy. So bright. So funny.

Lila bites her nails. She examines the painting.

LILA
It's signed Hall Hemingway.

MRS. HEMINGWAY
Hall was my maiden name. Women artists need strong names to compete with men. Grace Hemingway sounds so... wishy-washy.

LILA
So does Lila Violet Nobis. Violet's my mother's name. She wrote poetry.

MRS. HEMINGWAY
She's published?

Lila shakes her head "no."

LILA
She died eight years ago. I didn't know she wrote 'til after, when I found the candy box.

Lila fetches a candy box from a nearby work table and opens it. Mrs. Hemingway's hand gently plucks a fragile paper from the box. She unfolds a poem and reads silently.

LILA (CONT'D)
It's my mother's dream of a debutante ball, with me in a hoopskirt and a diamond tiara. A tiara. Imagine.

MRS. HEMINGWAY
She'd be proud you're in college.

LILA
Yes, ma'am. She fought to go to high school 'stead of working in a factory. Caused a scandal.

Mrs. H. smiles approvingly. Lila is encouraged.

LILA (CONT'D)
She wore gym bloomers and a middy blouse to play basketball. Another scandal.

MRS. HEMINGWAY
I wore gym bloomers and a middy blouse, too, in a class at the Y. Learned to kick over my head.

Lila puts the poem and the candy box back and chews her nails.

MRS. HEMINGWAY (CONT'D)
Are you nervous, dear?

LILA
Never thought I'd meet the mother of my literary idol. God.

MRS. HEMINGWAY
Don't say "God." A lady never takes the name of the Lord in vain. And stop biting your nails.

Lila hides her hands behind her back.

LILA
Yes, ma'am.

MRS. HEMINGWAY
Remember, you're a child of God. Only good can come to you.

LILA
My mother said that, too, and I believed it 'til -- strange...

For just a moment, she looks like she might cry, but quickly she's "Lila the Strong" again.

Mrs. Hemingway gives her a "What is it?" look.

LILA (CONT'D)
... I didn't cry when she died. Not then. Not since.

MRS. HEMINGWAY
Tears are salutary, dear.

Marcelline strolls from the cottage (holding the letters), dressed plainly as always, and watches unseen.

MRS. HEMINGWAY (CONT'D)
As for having a literary idol, when Aaron fashioned a golden calf to worship, God's wrath waxed hot.

MARCELLINE
And so will mine if you don't let Lila get back to work.

Lila takes the letters and manila envelope and races away.

INT. THE COTTAGE - KITCHEN - DAY

Marcelline clicks the lights on and off for Mrs. Hemingway.

MARCELLINE
Voila! Lights, a refrigerator, an electric iron. How did we manage without them?

MRS. HEMINGWAY
We said we liked roughing it.

MARCELLINE
We lied. You're sweet to help pay for this. And we love the rowboat.

MRS. HEMINGWAY
My pleasure. Too bad you and Ernie had that little tiff.

MARCELLINE
I only asked to borrow his boat for the children. And after all the years I've looked after Windemere.

Marcelline and Mrs. Hemingway move to the adjoining

LIVING ROOM

where Marcelline winds the mantel clock above the stone fireplace until it chimes. Mrs. Hemingway rocks in a chair.

MRS. HEMINGWAY
I'd like to see Windemere again. We had such good times....

MARCELLINE
It'd break your heart to see the old place now, Muzz. It's all boarded up and run down. Ernie's never used it. Not once.

Lila, minus her hat, serves iced tea and hovers.

MRS. HEMINGWAY
I have an idea about Ernie...
(sips her tea)
... And you. What if he showed up at Walloon... for his birthday?

Lila drops the wooden tray. She retrieves it and dutifully departs.

Marcelline, dismayed, speaks with strained courtesy.

MARCELLINE
I'd bake a cake. I'd be polite.

MRS. HEMINGWAY
I know. You're a good girl.

MARCELLINE
Ernie doesn't think so. That time I was in New York? He was there, too. I went to his hotel. He refused to see me.

Marcelline turns away, fighting tears.

MRS. HEMINGWAY
I'm sorry, dear. But this year -- since he's back from Spain -- he might surprise us.

MARCELLINE
Why? He hasn't been here in seventeen years.

Marcelline turns back and sees her mother's anguish.

MARCELLINE (CONT'D)
Why don't you write him and invite him, if that'll make you feel better.

MRS. HEMINGWAY
It would.

MARCELLINE
I'm giving a tea for you tomorrow, Muzz. You will sing for us?

Mrs. Hemingway spots a melodeon draped with a Spanish shawl near a viola and bow. She goes to it.

MRS. HEMINGWAY
Only for you, dear heart.

Mrs. Hemingway begins to play and sing a hymn.

SEPIA FLASHBACK - THE MELODEON

A younger Mrs. Hemingway continues to play and sing the same hymn.

Marcelline plays viola. Ernie plays his cello. And Dr. Hemingway plays his cornet.

Mrs. Hemingway is completely into her singing.

BACK TO THE COTTAGE LIVING ROOM

Mrs. Hemingway continues singing with the same expression as in the past. Marcelline only smiles at the sweet memory.

MARCELLINE
Such rousing times....

EXT. COTTAGE - BACK YARD - LATER

Lila, with canvas gloves and hat, stacks fireplace wood. Mrs. Hemingway's hymn can barely be heard.

WILLIS swaggers in from the road. In his late 30s, he looks like an Ernest Hemingway clone with moustache, but dresses and poses like an ad in Esquire.

Lila, startled, drops the logs she was holding. Willis grins.

LILA
Oh, God -- I mean, Oh gosh. Ernest?
Ernest Hemingway? Is that you?

She tries to bite her nails, but her gloves are still on.

WILLIS
You were expecting him?

LILA
No, yes, well, maybe. For his birthday.

WILLIS
'Fraid he's busy in Cuba this summer
... with a fellow war correspondent,
only she isn't a fellow.

LILA
That's just ugly gossip.

WILLIS
Oh? What do you care?

LILA
I admire his writing, that's all.

Lila stacks more wood. They talk across the woodpile.

WILLIS
You must be one of Marcelline's college
girls. What school?

LILA
Wayne State, in Detroit.

WILLIS
Oh. What sorority?

LILA
City colleges don't have sororities. They're such snobs.

WILLIS
I'm a Sigma Delta Chi man, myself.

LILA
Sooo?

WILLIS
So, what do you do at Wayne, besides study the Great Mister Hemingway?

LILA
Nothing to interest a fraternity man.

WILLIS
Try me.

LILA
I'm on the fencing team.

WILLIS
Really? I fence at The Salle -- that's a private club. Our instructor's world famous.

Willis demonstrates a couple of fencing moves sans foil.

LILA
He's our instructor, too. He works us hard. Some girls faint.

WILLIS
Not you.

LILA
Not me.

Lila picks up a log. Willis helps.

WILLIS
What else do you do at Wayne?

LILA
I organized a protest march against the Daughters of the American Revolution.

WILLIS
That was brash.

She shakes a log at Willis.

LILA
They deserved it. They wouldn't let Marian Anderson sing at Constitution Hall -- just 'cause she's a Negro. Imagine.

WILLIS
Imagine.

LILA
But Eleanor Roosevelt saved the day. She set up a concert in front of the Lincoln Memorial. Put the D-A-R in its place. Stupid women.

WILLIS
My mother belongs to the D-A-R.

LILA
Oh, I'm sorry. Unless she's the one who tried to get me expelled.

WILLIS
You and Ernie, a couple of rabble-rousers. 'Cept Ernie opposed Franco in Spain, an' Franco won.

LILA
But Ernest'll write a book about it. He'll win with words.

Lila picks up a log and jumps back. A garter snake slithers away.

WILLIS
You're supposed to scream like the girl last summer.

LILA
Silly girl.

Lila resumes stacking logs and kindling. But she keeps a lookout for other snakes.

WILLIS
You're no fun. Where's my pal, Marcelline?

LILA
Inside.

WILLIS
Good old Marce. She's the only one in Detroit society with any brains. Is that her new Ford at the road?

LILA
Mrs. Hemingway's.

WILLIS
The matriarch. Did you curtsy?

LILA
I felt like it. Mrs. Sanford's giving a tea for her tomorrow.

WILLIS
Better disappear 'til it's over. Tell Marce I'm up for the summer. Alone. I need her charming company.

LILA
I'll tell her.

WILLIS
And tell Carol I'll take her to see The Wizard of Oz when it opens.

Willis starts back up the road.

LILA
Wait. I don't know your name.

Willis returns, shakes her hand -- which is still encased in a canvas glove -- and holds it.

WILLIS
Willis Homer Whittemore.

Lila pulls her hand away.

LILA
You're the spitting image of Ernest.

WILLIS
And you're a charming waif in a Charlie Chaplin movie.

Lila picks up a tree branch, then a second one which she hands to Willis. She strikes a fencer's pose.

LILA
En-grade!

Willis, startled, laughs. He removes a few leaves from the branch, making it smooth.

He then sets it down, makes a show of taking off his jacket and hat, hanging it on a tree, and whipping the branch. His is the air of the master about to teach the novice a lesson.

WILLIS

En-grade.

Willis advances and lunges, but Lila parries. He lunges again, grinning.

They fence up and down the yard.

Willis leaps on a log. Lila jumps from a rock.

Willis backs up towards the house. Glances at

A WINDOW

which frames the three smiling faces of Mrs. Hemingway, teenaged CAROL, and Marcelline -- not seen by Lila.

Marcelline waves to Willis with a slight flick of her fingers.

BACK IN THE BACK YARD

Willis wags his head to Marcelline as if to say, "You ain't seen nothing yet." He boldly charges Lila, who sidesteps him. Then, with an upward lift of her branch, she knocks his branch from his hand.

Triumphant, Lila presses the tip of her branch against his chest as if to run it through his body. Grinning, she pulls back and salutes him, fencer-style, with her branch-foil.

Willis flushes with embarrassment. He glances at the window in time to see the curtains draw. He glowers.

WILLIS (CONT'D)

Beginners luck, young lady. But I'll be back, so beware.

Lila tosses her head and laughs.

Willis retrieves his coat and hat, and stomps to his car.

Lila takes the canvas gloves and rake to the shed.

INT. SHED

She pokes among the cobwebs. She gasps when she spots Ernest's lantern hanging overhead. She can't reach it, so she climbs on some old boxes and removes it carefully as if it were a religious relic.

She lays it outside the shed, then re-enters.

Excited, she rummages and finds a canvas heap that is obviously Ernest's old tent -- the same as in the photograph.

EXT. BACK YARD

Lila drags the tent out of the shed just as Marcelline calls from the stoop outside the kitchen door.

Lila whirls, picks up the lantern, and runs to Marcelline.

LILA
Look what I found, Mrs. Sanford.
Ernest's lantern. And his tent, too.

MARCELLINE
Put that lantern back. It's full of cobwebs. And the tent's rancid.

LILA
But I have this idea, this nifty idea. I want to live in Ernest's tent.

MARCELLINE
His tent's tattered. It leaks.

LILA
I'll fix it up.

MARCELLINE
Lila, I've worked hard to make this little place beautiful. I hand-picked every rock for the fireplace. I sanded and painted old furniture.
(presses her lips)
I don't want to look out at Ernie's ugly tent every time I turn around.

LILA
Yes, ma'am. But what if I put it in that clearing inside the woods where you'd never see it. Please?

Marcelline turns away and murmurs.

MARCELLINE
Ernie. Why always Ernie?

Marcelline turns back, takes a deep breath, and sees Lila's pleading look. Marcelline softens, sighs.

MARCELLINE (CONT'D)
Just keep the tent out of my sight. And no complaints when you freeze.

LILA
No, ma'am.

Marcelline turns away.

LILA (CONT'D)
Wait. Mr. Whittemore came by.

MARCELLINE
(feigns innocence)
Oh really?

LILA
Said he's here alone and needs your company -- your "charming company," he said.

MARCELLINE
Good. I could use his flattery.

She turns and walks back to the house.

EXT. CLEARING NEAR THE COTTAGE - DAY

Nearly dusk. Lila hammers the last wood tent stake into the ground. She fills an orange crate with a few Hemingway books.

Carol -- a shy, modest teenager and Marcelline's daughter -- timidly approaches from the cottage. She approaches Lila from behind. When Lila backs up to admire her work, she nearly backs into Carol.

CAROL
Ya really gonna sleep in that?
(peeks inside the tent)
Yuk. It smells moldy.

LILA
It'll air out.

CAROL
Mother says you'll move back to the cottage after you freeze a few nights.

LILA
I'll be warm as toast in this old Army blanket. Help me move this cot inside, Carol.

Lila and Carol move the cot and blanket

INSIDE THE TENT

where Carol grimaces at the smell and looks all around.

CAROL
Spooky.

LILA
Not spooky. Sacred.

CAROL
Sacred? Never heard of a tent being sacred.

LILA
Well, this one is, 'cause it was your Uncle Ernie's tent, his cot, his blanket, his lantern.

Carol and Lila duck

OUTSIDE THE TENT

where Lila becomes suddenly aware of something. She looks around. Shivers. Another mystical moment.

Carol brings her out of her trance.

CAROL
... And all your books were written by him. Don't you read anyone else?

LILA
Is there anyone else?

Lila drags the orange crate of books into the tent. Reappears.

CAROL
You're funny, Lila.

A sudden crash in the woods behind the tent sounds like an animal racing through the brush.

LILA
What was that?

They race towards the direction of the sound.

CAROL
Hoofprints. See?

Carol and Lila crouch to examine the hoofprints.

LILA
Like little arrows.
(standing)
That explains it. I had this eerie feeling of being watched, but... a deer. I've never seen a deer.

CAROL
You will.

Lila smiles at the thought. Stands.

LILA
If Ernest comes for his birthday, I'll show him I lived in his old tent.

CAROL
You're funny. Hope you're as good at camping as you are at fencing.

Lila looks puzzled while Carol jogs to the cottage.

Lila lights the kerosene lantern and swings it in front of the tent like a priest waving incense, giving a blessing.

She sets it down and she sits cross-legged on the ground near the pine tree, takes a journal from her pocket, and hunches over it -- writing.

LATER THAT NIGHT

Lila continues to write in her journal.

She stops to gaze at the fireflies blinking in the grass and trees. She holds an expression of wonder.

And then her stuttering whipporwill lands on a pine bough. The bird calls. "Whip whip. Whip poor, whip poor. Whippoorwill, whippoorwill."

Lila salutes the bird and smiles.

LILA
Soon I'll get my song right, too.

Lila resumes writing as the whipporwill continues singing.

INT. COTTAGE - SCREENED PORCH - CONTINUOUS

Marcelline types, pauses, hears the whippoorwill.

She turns off her lamp and walks to the screen, listening and looking fondly at the glow of the lantern in the trees until it is blown out.

And the fireflies continue their silent, mysterious dance.

FADE TO BLACK

FADE IN:

EXT. COTTAGE - FRONT YARD - DAY

Lila, in a white maid's apron, freshly pressed dress, and her red felt hat, wipes the lawn chairs.

Paper lanterns bob from cane poles, and paintings rest against tree trunks.

Carol hurries from the cottage, a serape over one shoulder. She carries Native American baskets and bowls, and Marcelline's viola and bow.

CAROL
Mother wants a New Mexican theme for the tea.

Lila helps Carol arrange the artifacts on a display table.

LILA
Very arty, Carol.

Willis, in his Chris Craft boat, approaches the dock, veers away, drives off, waving. Carol waves as he disappears.

LILA (CONT'D)
He seems very fond of you.

CAROL
If I tell you something, promise you won't tell Mother?

Lila quickly nods, sensing a secret about to be revealed.

CAROL (CONT'D)
Last summer, I had a crush on Willis.

LILA
Well-l-l, he's handsome in an older-man way, and girls your age --

CAROL
I'm more mature now.

LILA
Of course.

CAROL
Besides, he's married.

LILA
Oh.

Lila hides the impact of this. Carol glances around.

CAROL
Hey, let's move this sculpture where guests can see it better.

LILA
You move it. I'm afraid to.

Carol digs around a three-foot ceramic sculpture of a shy, nude, young woman and replants it in a bed of ferns.

LILA (CONT'D)
I've never seen a nude sculpture anywhere but in an art gallery. Who sculpted her?

CAROL
Mother. She studied in Paris.

LILA
In Paris? God.

CAROL
Mother says you're not to say "God."

LILA
In Paris? Holy Toledo...

Carol and Lila begin to hang paintings from tree limbs.

LILA (CONT'D)
... Your mother sculpts, acts, writes, plays the viola. Is there anything she doesn't do?

CAROL
You left out lectures.

LILA
Holy Toledo. Must come from being your Uncle Ernest's twin.

CAROL
Does not.

LILA
My professor said dressing Ernest as a girl was a threat to his masculinity.

CAROL
Bet he didn't tell you Mother had to wear boy's overalls and had a Dutch Boy haircut.

LILA
Well, no.

CAROL
Or that she was held back a year in school... just so he could start kindergarten at the same time.

LILA
Still, it must've been great being Ernest's best pal... and watching his talent develop.

CAROL
Mother is talented, too. They took turns, you know, editing their high school paper.

Lila steps back and holds out her arms to embrace the scene.

LILA
Carol. You've created an art gallery in the woods.

Enchanted, Lila strolls amid Mrs. Hemingway's paintings.

LILA (CONT'D)
Imagine. Trees blossoming with art. I'll write a poem about it.

CAROL
All you can think about is writing.

LILA
Wish I could write a story like your uncle's... the one about the blacksmith.

CAROL
Mother detests it.

LILA
See, this blacksmith comes in from deer hunting, and he stands behind this hired girl, and....

Lila moves her hands towards her breasts, but spots Marcelline and Mrs. H stroll from the cottage -- Marcelline in a customarily plain dress, Mrs. Hemingway in a New Mexican-style party gown. Carol gasps, still enraptured by the blacksmith story.

CAROL
On her --

Lila quickly whips off her hat, makes a deep bow. Carol turns to see her mother and hides a guilty look.

LILA
Welcome to the Walloon Institute of Art. Our curator, Miss Carol Sanford.

CAROL
You're funny.

Carol shyly accepts the applause. They tour the yard.

MARCELLINE
Looks lovely, Carol.

Mrs. Hemingway twirls so her skirt flares.

MRS. HEMINGWAY
Like my dress, girls? Designed for my Taos show. You should copy it Marce. You need more color in your wardrobe.

MARCELLINE
I'm not the ruffles type.

MRS. HEMINGWAY
Give me your measurements --

MARCELLINE
-- Mother. I don't want to copy your dress.

The mailman's car horn beeps several times from the road.

MARCELLINE (CONT'D)
Expecting a letter from Sterling.

Marcelline darts towards the road.

MRS. HEMINGWAY
Afraid I hurt your mother's feelings.

CAROL
Mother hasn't been well.

MRS. HEMINGWAY
But Walloon can heal anything.... Come show me that dancing school dress you'll wear to tea.

Carol and Mrs. Hemingway stroll into the cottage as Marcelline returns, reading a letter. She halts and calls frantically.

MARCELLINE
Lila? Lila, come here at once.

Lila flinches and runs to her. Marcelline shakes the letter.

MARCELLINE (CONT'D)
Why didn't you tell me your father forbade you to take this job?

LILA
Because it wasn't fair. I wanted this job desperately.

MARCELLINE
(reading the letter)
"Lila needs to help her step-mother, Nita, and the baby. And Thomas won't mind us. Instead, Lila works for rich, immoral people" -- shall I go on?

Lila clamps her hands over her ears.

LILA
No, no. I can't bear it when my father rants and raves like that.

MARCELLINE
(suddenly disarmed)
I know. My darling Daddy'd be laughing one minute and have us on our knees the next. With his leather belt.

LILA
My father's changed. After Mother died, he'd come home from Ford with his clothes smelling like oil and burnt metal. He'd put his lunch bucket on the table, and we'd make plans. He'd build a house, I'd write.
(bites her lips)
Then he began losing jobs and drinking too much. Then he married Nita. Then their baby came. Then ...

MARCELLINE
... you felt abandoned ... so you --

LILA
-- I thought Nita would stand up for me if I came here.

MARCELLINE
It can't be easy for her. A new marriage, a baby girl, two older step-children who are bonded.

LILA
Were bonded. At first when my mother died, I slept on the floor of Thomas's room. I was afraid he'd die, too.

MARCELLINE
And now?

LILA
He's the star basketball player in high school and I never see him. Thomas doesn't need me any more.

Marcelline slumps into a lawn chair. She takes it in, nods slightly in understanding, her face betraying the same feeling, like she and Lila are twins.

MARCELLINE
When Ernie became a reporter at the Kansas City Star, I felt left behind, too.
(snaps out of it)
Which doesn't change things, Lila. I counted on you, with my health. And to help so I could write my play. Now I'll have to send you home.

Lila sags to the grass. Marcelline touches her head.

MARCELLINE (CONT'D)
If I could think.

Marcelline stands, gestures to Lila, and the two walk towards the cottage.

INT. COTTAGE - SCREENED PORCH - CONTINUOUS

Marcelline steps through with Lila close behind.

MARCELLINE
Don't slam...

But it's too late. The door slams. Lila looks apologetic.

But just as quickly, Mrs. Hemingway and Carol (in her dancing school dress) dash through the door. It slams again.

Marcelline can only shrug in surrender.

AT MARCELLINE'S DESK AREA

Marcelline grabs a pad of paper.

MARCELLINE
What if I write your father? Assure him you've been working hard, saving money for tuition and --

LILA
-- Please, please. I'll do anything.

MARCELLINE
Get your head out of the clouds? And stop slamming the doors?

LILA
Cross my heart and hope to die.

MARCELLINE
And about Ernie. I've always defended him as a writer, but he's turning forty. If he shows up, I don't want you mooning after him.

LILA
I wouldn't moon after him.

MARCELLINE
You think not. But I remember how he left Hadley and their darling boy --

LILA
-- I'm only interested in his writing. I want to study what inspired him. To explore his mind.

MARCELLINE
That's a big order.

Lila grabs Marcelline's arm.

LILA
I can do it. Last winter, I walked in slush to save bus fare to buy his short stories and play.

MARCELLINE
(pensive, half-smiling)
I miss his wit.

LILA
I like his story where Nick Adams watches his doctor-father do a Caesarean section with a jack-knife.

MARCELLINE
Ernie's good with gore.

LILA
But the baby's father has committed suicide. On the way home, the doctor and Nick talk in those great, little sentences...

Marcelline looks reflective. .

LILA (O.S.) (CONT'D)
... About dying. And is it hard --

SEPIA FLASHBACK - HEMINGWAY'S KITCHEN - DECEMBER 6, 1928

-- A GUNSHOT truncates Mrs. Hemingway's singing.

Her hand hits the black metal scale. Apple slices fly everywhere.

She falls to her knees.

Her face -- mixed horror and confusion. She looks up toward the stairs.

BACK TO THE COTTAGE

Marcelline collapses in a chair, bows her head to her knees and sits quietly a long time. At last she lifts her head.

MARCELLINE
Our Daddy, Ernest's and mine, our Doctor-Daddy, shot himself to death.

LILA
Oh, I'd forgotten.

MARCELLINE
(smiles through tears)
My Daddy delivered me, his firstborn.

LILA
... I'm so sorry.

MARCELLINE
He'd call me his Marshmallow.

Marcelline spots her viola in the display. She drops the pad on the table and picks up the viola instinctively, starts to play, but it is out of tune. She begins to tune it.

MARCELLINE (CONT'D)
Ernie took over at the funeral. He was wonderful, just like old times.

SEPIA FLASHBACK - THE FUNERAL

-- Ernest confidently eulogizes his father MOS.

MARCELLINE (V.O.) (CONT'D)
Then we had a terrible quarrel. I stood up to Ernie...

-- Marcelline explains to an upset Ernest MOS. He is angry, says something, and marches out.

MARCELLINE (V.O.) (CONT'D)
I defended my daddy's last act. Daddy was sick -- his diabetes, bouts of depression. Money worries.

Marcelline wears a pained expression.

BACK TO THE COTTAGE

Marcelline carries the same pained expression. She looks up at Lila.

MARCELLINE (CONT'D)
I haven't seen Ernie since.

LILA
Ten years. Imagine.

Marcelline gets the viola tuned and starts playing a melancholy serenade. The viola sounds almost funeral, a musical echo of bittersweet memories that register on Marcelline's countenance as she plays.

LILA (CONT'D)
Maybe he'll come to his birthday.

With that happy thought, Marcelline changes to a upbeat number. A new memory.

SEPIA FLASHBACK - THE LAKE SHORE AT NIGHT

It's Ernie's eighth birthday. Signs and balloons are apparent. Directly next to Child Ernest stands a Birthday Tree with cards on it. Family members prepare Japanese lanterns.

CHILD MARCELLINE
If you're eight today, how old does that make me?

CHILD ERNEST
Nine.

Together they flatten the lanterns, light the candles, and float the lanterns onto the lake.

CHILD MARCELLINE
But I'm your twin -- shouldn't that make me the same age as you?

CHILD ERNEST
You're my <u>older</u> twin.

Everyone laughs.

The viola music slows in tempo as Child Ernest pushes a lantern onto the lake and gazes at it in wonder. Marcelline contentedly watches from behind.

CHILD MARCELLINE
There go the spirits of those who have died.

They both look solemnly at the lighted lanterns.

Ernie nods back at a cluster of Japanese lanterns on the shore, then to those drifting apart on the lake.

CHILD ERNEST
First they're together. Then they drift apart.

And the music has now segued to the former melancholy piece.

Marcelline's viola music then fades to the sounds of wind and water lapping on the lakeshore. The lanterns drift apart.

FADE TO BLACK.

FADE IN:

EXT. LAKESIDE - DAY

On a blustery morning, Lila rinses laundry in the lake.

Sheets billow. Lila falls, strips off her soaked dress, laughs, and splashes with abandon.

Loons skim the water and take flight, with Lila chasing them as if they were playmates.

EXT. COTTAGE - BACK YARD - LATER

In her demure, wet underwear, Lila hangs laundry on a line. It FLAPS in the wind. She snatches her journal.

Willis wanders in from the road, carrying a picnic hamper and jug of wine. Bemused, he watches, unseen.

LILA
(reading her journal)
"The sweep, sweep of the waves, the leaves shivering like distant tambourines. Did they give Ernest the tempo for his writing? This stand of birch, that point of land..."

WILLIS
Hello, there.

LILA
Oh, Mister... Whittemore.

WILLIS
Call me Willis. And you never told me your name.

LILA
Lila. Lila Violet Nobis.

WILLIS
Well, Lila Violet Nobis. Hoped to see you again ... but not to see so much of you.

She looks at her undress and gasps.

She races into her tent to dress. Willis glimpses the tent, then sets the hamper and wine on the picnic table nearby.

INT. TENT

Lila throws on some clothes.

LILA
How dare you sneak up like that?

EXT. TENT

Willis pulls picnic items out of the hamper and begins setting the table.

WILLIS
I didn't sneak up. I came upon --

LILA (O.S.)
Nobody's home, so I....

WILLIS
Where's everyone?

LILA (O.S.)
Boys're at camp. Carol's with a friend. Women went shopping for the Fourth of July. A big wingding.

WILLIS
Hemingways are big on wingdings.

Lila, dressed, emerges from the tent. Her red felt hat flies off in the wind.

Willis looks away to hide his smile as she chases it.

WILLIS (CONT'D)
Heard you spouting about Ernie.

LILA
So.

WILLIS
And you look swell in wet underwear. What if I tell Marcelline?

Lila wheels around and scolds.

LILA
Don't you dare.
(fondly recalling)
Besides, it was beautiful, with the sheets billowing up ... like clouds fallen in the lake.

WILLIS
Do I hear a poem in the making? Girls like you usually write poems.

LILA
Yes, I'll write a poem. 'Cause when I waded into the water, I felt... baptized. So spare me your smutty remarks about my underwear.

Willis fixes bread and cheese.

WILLIS
Sorry. Thought you were more sophisticated. I'm starving. How 'bout you?

LILA
Too busy. What time is it?

Willis holds up his wristwatch. Lila touches his arm to look. He clasps her hand and she jumps away.

LILA (CONT'D)
It's late. God. I mean, gosh.

WILLIS
Gosh?

LILA
Mrs. Hemingway says not to say... well, I keep forgetting.

Lila shoves carrots and a scraper to Willis from a pan on the picnic table. He sips his wine. Lila peels potatoes.

WILLIS
Well, gosh. I don't know how to clean carrots.

LILA
You're useless.

WILLIS
That's what my wife, Bonnie, says. My soon-to-be ex-wife. We're getting a divorce.

Lila is momentarily stunned.

LILA
Peel the carrots down this way

WILLIS
My boy's only four and he speaks French! He's in Paris with Bonnie. Her idea of a last party 'fore the big war.

LILA
Aren't you scared with Hitler rattling around? Mrs. Sanford's worried 'bout Ernest's wife, Pauline, over there.

WILLIS
Ernie's not worried. Here. Relax. Have some wine.

Willis pours a second glass. Offers it to Lila.

LILA
No, thanks. I'm not sophisticated, remember?

WILLIS
You're so serious. And bossy.

LILA
That's what Thomas says -- my kid brother.

Willis cuts his thumb with the scraper. Swears under his breath.

LILA (CONT'D)
Ernie knew how to peel carrots, and filet fish and --

WILLIS
Tell me, why you're hooked on Ernie?

LILA
What do you care? You think it's silly for "girls like me" to write poetry.

Willis shrugs, sips his wine, adds more.

LILA (CONT'D)
But if you must know, I'm gonna be a famous writer and I need to know what Ernest knows.
(she counters)
Why're you hooked on him?

WILLIS
He's a great friend to his friends. Great hunter, skier, fisherman. Do you fish?

LILA
Never tried it.

WILLIS
Can't know what Ernie knows 'less you know how to fish. Could pick you up some morning at five. It's so still, if a fish splashes, you jump.

LILA
Like Nick Adams fishing in Ernest's "Big Two-Hearted River."
(gazes at the lake)
I wonder what it'd be like. As you said, so still. And not sure what to expect...

Willis looks at her fondly. She gazes up at him. The moment is romantically charged.

WILLIS
... Because it's your first time.

LILA
Yes....

She pauses, embarrassed, and shyly turns her head away from him.

He kindly breaks the moment for her, turning from the romantic to the intellectual.

WILLIS
Hey, you really know Ernie's work.

LILA
Study it line for line. Wish I had "Death in the Afternoon."

WILLIS
His bullfighting book? Never heard of a girl who likes --

LILA
-- Stop calling me a girl. I'm twenty-one. And it's about more than bullfighting.

WILLIS
What's Marcelline up to these days?

LILA
Writing a play about the young Hemingways. Walloon brings back the memories --

WILLIS

Like what?

LILA

Like when she first baked a mahogany cake. Mr. Sanford said he'd marry the girl who baked it.

WILLIS

How delicious.

LILA

Holy Toledo. It's clouding up. Better get these clothes inside.

Lila puts the laundry on the porch and returns just as Marcelline and Mrs. Hemingway rush into the yard with packages. They go to Willis, hug him.

MARCELLINE

About time you visited, Willis. I didn't expect to find you scraping carrots.

WILLIS

Lila made me do it.

MARCELLINE

I guess you've given up fencing?

Lila helps Mrs. Hemingway take packages into the cottage.

WILLIS

Touche.... Lila tells me you're writing a play 'bout your romance -- a piece of cake.

MARCELLINE

(suspicions aroused)

You two must have had quite a chat.

WILLIS

She amused me with Ernie's quotes. I promised to teach her to fish. Sunday morning at five?

MARCELLINE

How is Bonnie? Is she with you?

WILLIS

She's still in Europe with our son.

MARCELLINE

Shouldn't you be there in case...?

WILLIS
I need time alone.

Marcelline frowns. Willis, uneasy, changes the subject.

WILLIS (CONT'D)
I better put up the top on my convertible. You know how fast storms hit at Walloon.

Willis rushes to the road.

INT. COTTAGE - SCREENED PORCH - DAY

Mrs. Hemingway and Lila unpack July Fourth decorations as Marcelline saunters in.

A quick flash of sheet lightning in the distance is followed by a low RUMBLE of thunder, signaling a storm.

MARCELLINE
If the power goes out, we'll have to eat cold food by candlelight.

MRS. HEMINGWAY
Like old times. Ernie loved storms. Poor boy. Last time I saw him, his eyes were so sad. But I have an idea.

Mrs. Hemingway pats Marcelline's arm affectionately.

MRS. HEMINGWAY (CONT'D)
I thought since Sterling's coming for the Fourth, when he goes back to the city, you could drive back with him.

MARCELLINE
Just Sterling and me?

MRS. HEMINGWAY
I can look after things here. And while you're gone... Ernie can come to Walloon and visit me. It would remove the strain on everyone.

Marcelline, stunned, fights tears.

MARCELLINE
Was that Ernie's idea. Or yours?

MRS. HEMINGWAY
It... it seemed sensible.

Marcelline holds Mrs. Hemingway's face in her hands like a mother scolding a child.

Another roll of thunder.

MARCELLINE
Mother, listen. Ernie has a yacht, a fancy house and pool. He summers on a ranch.

Tears flow as Marcelline speaks.

MARCELLINE (CONT'D)
This cottage is all I have. I won't leave it to please your sad-eyed son.

Marcelline takes down her hands, clenches them.

MARCELLINE (CONT'D)
It's the meanest thing I've ever heard.

MRS. HEMINGWAY
I didn't mean to make you cry.

MARCELLINE
Well, you did.

MRS. HEMINGWAY
I don't want my twins to quarrel.

Marcelline turns her back to her mother. A flash of light.

MARCELLINE
Tell that to your son. I've written him very kind letters about Walloon. Said I hoped to see him and his family here... and what do I get?

MRS. HEMINGWAY
Please, dear. I...

But there's no stopping Marcelline now. The thunder rolls.

MARCELLINE
He humiliates me. Says sarcastic things 'cause I went to college and he didn't. He brings up things from years ago. Still, I was willing to invite him here for his birthday.

MRS. HEMINGWAY
I know, dear, but --

MARCELLINE
(turns back)
-- Ernie's changed. I don't know him anymore.
(MORE)

MARCELLINE (CONT'D)
(a swift dagger)
Why don't you go to Cuba, Mother, if that's where your heart is?

Mrs. Hemingway bravely takes the blow. Indignant, she holds her head high and marches to her room. A gust of wind follows her. She slams the door shut.

Outside, trees bend to the wind as the first drops of rain fall, followed by a loud clap of thunder.

Marcelline goes to

THE KITCHEN

where she struggles to calm herself as she watches Lila arrange vegetables around a roast in an electric pan.

MARCELLINE (CONT'D)
Lila... that extra wine glass?

LILA
Willis, I mean, Mr. Whittemore, he offered me a drink. I refused.

MARCELLINE
(pointedly)
And about that fishing trip. No, you can't go with him.

LILA
I know.

MARCELLINE
Mother and I bought you some mosquito netting. No use getting eaten alive.

LILA
Thanks. I hate to admit it, but --

Lila starts chewing her nails.

MARCELLINE
And that package in the mail? It's a pair of shorts. Nita sent them. Write a thank-you note. Learn some social graces.

Lila throws her hands behind her.

LILA
Was there a letter?

MARCELLINE
Your brother and father quarrel. The baby is teething and cries.

LILA
Why doesn't she rock her? Sing to her? I made up songs and they said I spoiled her. You don't spoil a baby by singing.

Lightning CRACKLES and thunder RUMBLES.

MARCELLINE
Bring candles and matches, Lila. We may need them.

THE LIVING ROOM - LATER

Willis sips wine and reads the play. More thunder. Lila sets candles around and clicks on lamps.

Marcelline sees Lila and Willis exchange glances. Lila darts to the window -- the sky is dark.

LILA
This storm's really keen.

MARCELLINE
Won't be "keen" when your tent floods.

Marcelline stretches out on the sofa. Willis leaps from his chair, waving her manuscript.

WILLIS
Your play's terrific, Mar-cel-line. And you're full of secrets. I never knew they called you Maz-a-ween.

MARCELLINE
Ernie couldn't pronounce his L's. The little ones copied him. But don't you dare tell our friends.

WILLIS
I won't, Maz-a-ween.

Willis ducks when Marcelline playfully throws a pillow at him.

WILLIS (CONT'D)
Just teasing. Lila, come read this scene with me. It's about baby Carol. I'm Sterling, you're Maz-a-ween. I mean, Mar-cel-line.

LILA
No, really. I don't want --

WILLIS
Here. Tuck this pillow to your shoulder and pretend it's the baby.

MARCELLINE
(sits bolt upright)
Willis, really, this is very improper. Lila works here, and you're a guest.

WILLIS
Aw, come on, Maaz. Be a good sport.

Willis holds out the manuscript to Lila, who shrinks back.

WILLIS (CONT'D)
I won't bite you. Now, I'm Sterling. I say: Baby Carol's a sweetheart, a beauty. Just like you Marcelline.

LILA
(reluctantly reads)
I... I... want Carol... to have the girlhood I had. Music, parties, dances, beaus.

She holds the pillow more naturally like a baby now.

WILLIC
Good, Lila. Go on.

LILA
I want her to have my heavenly summers at Walloon... canoeing, skeet shooting, toasting marshmallows around a campfire.
(looks at the pillow)
There, there. Don't cry, little baby.

Lila, unwittingly caught up in the drama, pats the pillow with her free hand and bursts into a "made-up" lullaby, as if singing to Nita's baby.

LILA (CONT'D)
"Baby Princess, from afar, in a velvet robe sprinkled with stars...."

Lila looks down at Willis's pillow, which is now...

SEPIA FLASHBACK - LILA'S HOME

...Nita's baby. Lila, wearing old clothes and her red felt hat, rocks the baby singing the same lullabye.

THOMAS -- age 16, tall, and holding a basketball -- steps into the room as if drawn by the lullabye.

LILA (CONT'D)
Come here, Thomas.

Thomas bounces the basketball once and walks up to her as she sings to the baby.

He kneels, lays down the basketball, and gently strokes the baby's cheek. He smiles at Lila, who pats his shoulder.

BACK TO THE COTTAGE LIVING ROOM

LILA (CONT'D)
"... Winking here, twinkling there.
Sleep, sleep, Baby Princess."

Willis tilts Lila's chin, kisses her lips, then turns abruptly away.

Lila, in shock, reaches to draw him back.

Marcelline, stunned, leaps from the sofa.

MARCELLINE
Willis, how dare you? Where do you think you are? This is my home. This girl is in my care.

Willis cowers, so Marcelline turns on Lila.

MARCELLINE (CONT'D)
And you, Lila. I thought you didn't want a beau. Seems I was wrong.

A loud CLAP of thunder is followed by a deluge of rain.

Lila runs out the door as the power goes off. Willis strikes a match and lights a candle.

WILLIS
I'm sorry, Marce. Guess I forgot myself and over-acted.

She glares at Willis who takes a last gulp of his wine.

MARCELLINE
It's a big responsibility to care for a naive young woman like Lila.

WILLIS
(sheepish)
I know.

MARCELLINE
She'll freeze in that stupid tent. Serves her right.

WILLIS

Take it easy, Maaz. See you.

Willis slips outside with an umbrella.

Marcelline struggles with her anger, rubbing her temples with her fingers. A CLAP of thunder reminds her of the storm outside.

She turns her face toward the door with sudden compassion, shaking her head.

EXT. COTTAGE - MOMENTS LATER

Another CLAP of thunder. Marcelline emerges in rain coat, galoshes and umbrella. She hugs a folded blanket. As the rain slows, she dashes through puddles toward Lila's lantern-lit tent.

EXT. TENT - CONTINUOUS

Marcelline hovers outside the tent, closes the umbrella and hunches over the blanket as her hair gets drenched.

MARCELLINE

Lila, you all right in there?

LILA

Yes, ma'am.

SEPIA FLASHBACK - INSIDE THE TENT

Teenaged Marcelline, 17, enters the tent and sees Teenaged Ernest, 16, shivering on his cot.

TEENAGED MARCELLINE

Ernie.

Ernest shakes his head.

TEENAGED MARCELLINE (CONT'D)

Well if you won't come inside....

Marcelline unfolds the blanket and tucks it around his shoulders.

TEENAGED ERNEST

Thanks, Marce.

PRESENT DAY - INSIDE THE TENT

Marcelline, 41 again, tucks the blanket around Lila's shoulders.

Lila turns to Marcelline -- surprised -- and grateful for her kindness.

MARCELLINE
If I'm too protective sometimes, it's only 'cause I know how easily --

LILA
-- I shouldn't have sung.

Marcelline sits on a nail keg used as a stool.

MARCELLINE
Willis still shouldn't have kissed you.

Lila snuggles under the blanket.

MARCELLINE (CONT'D)
The play needs rewriting.

LILA
Don't change the romance. It must have been wonderful to be in love at Walloon. To get engaged here.

MARCELLINE
Yes. But Walloon can break your heart, too. So be careful.

LILA
I can't think about love. My writing.

MARCELLINE
Of course.

Lila leans forward, face to face with Marcelline.

LILA
Mrs. Sanford, could you talk to your mother about... everything?

MARCELLINE
Yes. I could. Why?

Lila looks away a moment -- trying to contain her heart's secret which insists on revealing itself.

LILA
'Cause I need my mother -- my real mother. I need her and I'm angry with her for leaving me. Imagine being angry at your dead mother.

Lila's chin quivers -- perhaps from the chill, perhaps from the longing.

MARCELLINE
I was angry at my father for dying. He never knew my little boys. He'd have taught them to hunt an' fish an' help people in need -- Daddy was good at that.

They reach toward each other and hug, sharing twin feelings.

MARCELLINE (CONT'D)
Would you like to sleep in the cottage?

LILA
I'm fine. I'll write about the storm.

MARCELLINE
Write about your anger at your mother.

Marcelline's face shows that she's saying this to herself.

EXT. TENT

Marcelline runs out into the rain and enters the cottage.

INTERCUT - MARCELLINE IN LIVING ROOM/LILA IN TENT

-- Marcelline has moved the typewriter into the living room. By candlelight, she types. The mantel clock CHIMES "Two a.m." She smiles, and blows out the candle.

-- Lila, in her tent, writes furiously. She smiles and blows out the lantern at the same moment that Marcelline blows out the candle.

FADE TO BLACK.

FADE IN:

Dawn on Walloon Lake. Golden light. Tranquility.

Carol and Mrs. Hemingway, with parasol, saunter to the dock.

INT. SCREENED PORCH - DAY

Marcelline types as Lila, in a life jacket, reads some pages.

LILA
I like your graduation speech on "The New Girlhood" -- that was bold.

MARCELLINE
A lot of high-flown idealism, I'm afraid.

Carol and Mrs. Hemingway call "Lila," "Hurry," from the dock.

EXT. DOCK - CONTINUOUS

Lila and Marcelline hurry to the dock. Lila climbs in at the oars with Carol in front, Mrs. Hemingway in back with a parasol.

MRS. HEMINGWAY
Marcelline, come with us. You're working too hard on your writing, dear.

MARCELLINE
I better stay with it, Muzz.

MRS. HEMINGWAY
I'm afraid you're trying to be too much like Ernie.

This turns Marcelline's countenance to stone.

MARCELLINE
You're the one who raised us as twins. You wanted us to be completely alike. It's rather late to want us to be completely different.

Mrs. Hemingway winces. Marcelline, looking grim, stalks back to the

SCREENED PORCH

where she starts typing, then throws her arms over the typewriter and bows her head on her arms.

EXT. WALLOON LAKE

Lila, Mrs. H, and Carol row past sand banks and bulrushes where orioles teeter and sing. Water lilies bloom. Willow trees wave gently.

Lila suddenly swings the rowboat toward a wooded bluff.

LILA
Thought something moved on that bluff.

CAROL
Still looking for your deer? You're funny.

But Lila has spotted something.

LILA
Windemere.

Windemere looms like a shabby spectre -- a once-white, boarded-up cottage with a separate dormitory. Mrs. Hemingway starts to stand and rocks the boat. She plops back down.

Lila nudges the rowboat ashore.

EXT. WINDEMERE

Carol scrambles up the rise. Lila and Mrs. Hemingway follow, picking their way through vines and debris.

MRS. HEMINGWAY
I remember the beach as wider, a green lawn.

LILA
You raised a great writer here.

Mrs. Hemingway takes heart, given her tiff with Marcelline.

MRS. HEMINGWAY
I raised a great family here.

LILA
Ernie stayed one winter alone to write, didn't he?

MRS. HEMINGWAY
Yes. But he moved to a rooming house in Petoskey when winter closed in.

LILA
And later, he honeymooned here?

MRS. HEMINGWAY
Yes. He and Hadley married in a church over in Horton Bay. That's the last time he was here.

Lila strokes the cottage door as if it were an historic monument.

MRS. HEMINGWAY (CONT'D)
When Ernie comes for his birthday, he'll restore Windemere. Bring his sons.

Mrs. Hemingway gets misty.

MRS. HEMINGWAY (CONT'D)
We'll all be happy again.

LILA
Don't cry, Mrs. Hemingway. Ernest'll come. You'll see.

MRS. HEMINGWAY
Pray so. As Job says, "My days are swifter than a weaver's shuttle."

Mrs. Hemingway sits on the porch steps, Carol beside her. Lila wanders off into the woods, looking for deer hoofprints.

Suddenly she glimpses A BOY about nine years old (a real boy, not a dream), in a floppy straw hat and ragged overalls. He carries a fishing pole and saunters to the shore.

Lila trails him. He brushes aside some branches, splashes in the water, tosses his fishing rod into a rickety rowboat and shoves off. He fishes in some lily pads.

Lila shoves aside the same branches and looks after him. She reaches toward him and calls softly.

LILA
Ernest?

But he keeps walking.

She stands transfixed, then runs down the beach to the Sanford rowboat. She waves to Mrs. Hemingway and Carol, and the three climb in and shove off.

Mrs. Hemingway glances back wistfully, dabs her eyes.

PRE-LAP - The SOUND of fireworks.

EXT. WALLOON LAKESHORE - NIGHT

Fireworks BOOM, sparks shower down. Cottagers "ooh" and "aah."

Lila stands back from the crowd, watching, as Willis arrives from the road and stands behind her, holding a book. He taps her shoulder. She turns, sees him, leaps away.

LILA
You almost missed the fireworks.

WILLIS
Had important business in Detroit. I've ordered a Piper Cub so I can fly back and forth 'stead of driving.

LILA
Among other things, you fly.

WILLIS
'Course. And I brought you this book of Ernie's from the library in my river house. For the only girl -- <u>woman</u> -- who likes bullfighting.

A BURST of fireworks provides light as Lila, dazed, examines the book.

LILA
"Death in the Afternoon"!
(turns to title page)
And it's autographed. "E. Hemingway, 1932." Holy Toledo!

She throws her arms around Willis, then quickly pulls away, embarrassed.

WILLIS
Actually, that's Holy Pamplona.

Lila appreciates the humor.

WILLIS (CONT'D)
It's my apology for... you know.

Lila finds a photograph of a little boy inserted in the book. Willis grabs it.

LILA
Who's that?

WILLIS
Oh! My little boy. Brought it along to keep me company.

LILA
The little boy who speaks French.

Willis pockets the photo. Lila hangs her head, clings to the book.

LILA (CONT'D)
Thank you, Willis.

He gestures "You're welcome." Lila runs with the book to her tent, while Willis gazes at the smoke-streaked sky.

The sounds of the cottagers gradually soften into silence while the smoke and clouds in the sky fade away into a clear, starry sky. The calls of loons are the only sound.

EXT. TENT - NIGHT

Lila sits cross-legged, listening and writing. The lantern is nearby. She looks across the black lake and then up at the starry sky.

EXT. WILLIS'S ROOM - SAME

Through an open window, Willis lies on a bed with his hands behind his head, listening to the same loons.

He grabs the photo of his son and looks at it.

FADE TO BLACK.

FADE IN:

EXT. WALLOON LAKE - DAY - A WEEK LATER

A Chris Craft eases across the water. Willis cuts the engine and drifts towards the dock.

Lila practices casting with a rickety fishing rod. She wears a new shorts-and-shirt outfit and sandals.

Willis watches her unseen.

As Lila flings her line backward, it snags behind her in a birch tree.

LILA
Oh, darn. Darn, darn, darn.

Lila jerks the line free and rewinds.

WILLIS
You'll never catch a bass that way.

LILA
Will, too. I'll catch a birch bass.

WILLIS
Birch bass?

LILA
They spawn in birch trees. Like poplar bass spawn in poplar trees, but they died out. Too poplar.

They laugh at Lila's joke.

WILLIS
Why not stand on the dock and cast into the lake, 'stead of the dirt?

LILA
'Cause I'm baking a mahogany cake.

She nods towards the cottage.

WILLIS
Not a replica of the cake that snagged Mr. Sanford.

Lila nods -- the very one.

WILLIS (CONT'D)
Where is Marcelline-Mazaween?

LILA
Shopping for Ernest's birthday.

WILLIS
Maaz gives wonderful parties, but she's wasting her time. That old rascal won't show up.

He looks over her fishing rod.

LILA
Will, too. Mrs. Hemingway phoned Cuba. The houseboy said Ernest's on a little trip -- a surprise. She figures he'll come by train from Miami to Petoskey, and then drive to --

WILLIS
-- Where in Creation did you get this rickety rod?

LILA
The shed.

WILLIS
Well, it needs oiling. A new line. Here. Hold your thumb.... No, no. Like this.

Willis stands behind Lila, circles her with his arms, and grips her hand as she holds the fishing rod. She pulls away.

LILA
I'll do it myself.

WILLIS
Bet you can't. Now, back, back. Then spring your arm forward. Easy. Easy.

Lila's line loops ahead and lands perfectly in the dirt. She jumps up and down, then reels in the line.

LILA
I did it, Willis. Watch out bass, watch out pike. Here I come.

Willis, irritated by her success, sips from his flask as Lila continues to practice casting, with occasional snags.

WILLIS
When you fish, remember to keep your eye on the sky. Red sky in mornin', sailors take warnin'.

LILA
... Red sun at night, sailor's delight. Mrs. Sanford knows those sayings. Her father taught her. Did your father teach you the stars?

WILLIS
No. Hardly knew him. An auto magnate, the papers called him. Impressed?

LILA
Hardly. My father's in the union. I grew up singing "Solidarity Forever" in the Labor Day parades.

WILLIS
Unions gave my father apoplexy.

LILA
Good.

WILLIS
He died.

LILA
Sorry. I didn't mean it that way.

WILLIS
Never knew my globe-trotting mother, either. She sent me to summer camps and boarding schools.

LILA
Wish my brother Thomas went to boarding school.

WILLIS
Got kicked out of two boarding schools. Then I discovered Ernie. Got hooked on American writers. At the University of Michigan --

LILA
You went to U. of M.? G-gosh. They have a literary magazine, a writing contest and...

WILLIS
... A football team, saloons, and great professors. One of 'em said I should get my master's, even my doctorate... and teach American Lit.

LILA
Why didn't you?

WILLIS
Family said I should see the world first. I looked up Ernie's haunts in Paris -- Michauds, The Cafe de la Paix. I skied at Chamby --

LILA
-- and Shruns? You skied at Shruns?

WILLIS
At Shruns. Then Father died. I came home, married, slid into managing the family estate.

Willis takes another drink from his flask.

LILA
But how could you give up teaching?

WILLIS
Might not have, if I'd grown up with a family like Ernie's.

LILA
We're twin orphans, you and I, envying the Hemingways.

Willis reaches to stroke her face, stops, drops his arm.

WILLIS
Hear the loons last night?

LILA
I wrote a poem about 'em. It's called Waiting for Mahn-go-Taysee." That's from Hiawatha. It means "Loon-hearted One."

WILLIS
I know. I went to Camp Mahn-go-Taysee.

LILA
Is there anything you haven't done?

EXT. LILA'S TENT

Lila gets her journal from her tent, now a campground with collected rocks and shells. She's made a table from driftwood, a bench from barn wood.

From a limb hangs a dreamcatcher -- a thin twig twisted like a hoop, webbed with string, and decorated with bird feathers and beads.

Willis, beside Lila on the bench, twirls the dreamcatcher.

WILLIS
We made dreamcatchers like this at camp. Snag any good dreams?

LILA
A few. -- Ah, here's my loon poem. It's by L.V. Nobis. Lila Violet is so wishy-washy. Women need strong names to compete with men.

WILLIS
Okay, L.V.-the-Strong. Read on.

LILA
"I first glimpsed you 'gainst a rose and saffron sky, yodeling at night. You laughed, cried like a child as I spread sacred herbs on your shore to draw you, my protector myth. When I shed this life, you'll come for me. We'll skim the treetops chorusing with wild abandon."

WILLIS
Who is your loon?

LILA
Just a loon. A spirit.

WILLIS
You're afraid. You want the wild abandon but you're afraid of love. You don't know anything about it.

LILA
Do, too.

WILLIS
From books? Is that where Ernie learned? You have to taste life, L.V. Get --

LILA
-- In my poem --

WILLIS
-- you hold life off 'til you die. Then someone carries you off and teaches you to love.

LILA
But --

WILLIS
-- If you must know, your poem is sentimental.

LILA
(leaps from bench)
That's the worst thing a poem can be. That's what people write who can't write.

WILLIS
Oh, hell. Now you'll cry and --

LILA
-- I'm too angry to cry.

She throws down her journal. Willis gives it back to her.

WILLIS
Stop that. Listen, L.V. You're a bright young woman but you go to a dumb city college --

LILA
That's an insult. We don't have a great football team, but we --

WILLIS
-- Bonnie went to Wellesley. Look. That could be you.

Willis shows her a wallet photo.

LILA
Could never be me. She's wearing a fur. And if Ford goes on strike, my family'll need my tuition money.

Willis puts the photo back and drinks again from his flask.

WILLIS
You could get a scholarship. Girls like you do that. Or... work for me... like you work for Mazaween.

LILA
You -- you're out of your mind.

WILLIS
It's your fault, with your loon and getting me excited about writers again. And I do want to help you.

LILA
I just want to write like Ernest.

WILLIS
Truly? Then grow up. Reach higher.

LILA
I don't know how. This is the most I've had. This place, these people.
(realizing)
They should be back soon. Did you bring the records for Carol?

WILLIS
Damn. Come with me to get 'em in my Chris Craft, 'stead of baking your damned cake.

LILA
The cake.

Lila rushes into the cottage.

A MOMENT LATER

She emerges with a charred, smoking, cake pan.

Willis laughs, dumps the cake and buries it.

WILLIS
A new recipe. Burnt Mahogany.

Lila, anguished, smacks him over the head with the cake pan.

LILA
But I wanted to please Mrs. Sanford. It's all your fault.

WILLIS
Dammit, don't be so serious. I'll get the records and we can dance. You do dance, don't you?

Lila shakes her head "no."

WILLIS (CONT'D)
Somehow I knew you didn't. Well, adieu.

Willis storms to the dock, guns his boat motor and roars off.

INT. COTTAGE - SCREENED PORCH - LATER

Lila and Marcelline unpack party favors. Lila's gift folder of poems for Ernest lies on an end table.

MARCELLINE
What smells? Did something burn?

LILA
A mahogany cake. It was to be a surprise.

MARCELLINE
I'm surprised.

LILA
Willis, I mean Mr. Whittemore, came by
and I forgot.

Marcelline turns Lila to face her and lectures.

MARCELLINE
He mustn't distract you.

LILA
We had a fight. He criticized my poem.
Says I should grow up.

MARCELLINE
So should he.

LILA
Says I should go to Wellesley.

MARCELLINE
Lila! Men like Willis sometimes try
to impress young women like you...
women in a different social class.
But they're only -- be careful.

LILA
Yes, ma'am.

Lila opens a package of Japanese lanterns and looks baffled.

MARCELLINE
For tomorrow's birthday. Japanese
lanterns. Ernie loved to float 'em on
the lake at night. Ordered 'em special.

Marcelline puts her hand to her head -- a headache. She sits down and picks up Lila's folder of poems, reads title.

MARCELLINE (CONT'D)
"Poems by Candlelight" by L.V. Nobis.
L.V.?

LILA
My pen-name. The poems are my birthday
gift to Ernest. At night when I light
his lantern, I feel like I'm lighting
a candle in church.

Marcelline rolls her eyes with an "give me a break" look.

MARCELLINE
I must lie down.

Carol enters the porch, winds the Victrola, and swing music BLARES. Marcelline puts down the folder and enters the house.

Carol takes Lila's hands and coaxes her to dance.

CAROL
Come on, Lila. Willis wants me to teach you to dance for the party. He's got a crush on you.

LILA
Has not.

CAROL
And you've got a crush on him.

LILA
Have not.

CAROL
You're funny.
(the teacher)
Okay, swing a little, sway a little. Forward, back. Slow, slow, quick-quick.

Lila's heart is not in it. Carol drops Lila's hand and takes the needle off the record.

CAROL (CONT'D)
You're no fun anymore. I don't know why Willis wants to dance with you.

LILA
Neither do I.

INT. COTTAGE - KITCHEN/LIVING - NIGHT

Marcelline smiles at the cake pan with burnt fragments in it. She walks into the living room -- a sweet memory in her head -- and lies down on the couch.

SEPIA FLASHBACK - WINDEMERE KITCHEN

YOUNG WOMAN MARCELLINE puts the finishing touches on her famous mahogany cake. She takes a deep breath -- a bit nervous -- and carefully carries the cake, backing through the door into

THE WINDEMERE MAIN ROOM (SEPIA FLASHBACK CONT'D)

where she kneels at the coffee table, trying to keep the cake level as she sets it down.

She hears voices of people approaching the cottage. She quickly stands and primps to an imaginary mirror.

She turns and there is a handsome STERLING. He glances at the cake, admires it, and Marcelline smiles shyly.

BACK TO THE COTTAGE LIVING ROOM

Marcelline's two hands are placed beside her face, like a baby sleeping, except her dream is a waking dream of her beloved Sterling.

EXT./INT. TENT - CONTINUOUS

Lila steps into the tent with her birthday folder of poems. She places a ribbon around it and then steps outside.

She kneels at the driftwood table-altar and places her folder on it as if making an offering. She lights a candle, still kneeling. She closes her eyes.

LILA

Mother-spirit, come to me. Help me say the right thing when Ernest comes tomorrow. Help him to like my poems.

She opens her eyes.

EXT. COTTAGE - FRONT YARD - DAY

Lila opens her eyes. She now wears heavy lipstick and a barrotto in her obviously curled hair. Her apron is starched.

Carol strings lanterns as Mrs. Hemingway joyfully arranges a table with a linen cloth, crystal punch bowl set, and a glass-domed dish holding the birthday cake.

Lila helps Marcelline deck a fir tree with party streamers and paper chains. She rubs her hand -- she's nervous. Marcelline twists her hair -- she's nervous.

A guest hangs a greeting card on one of the branches.

MARCELLINE

You look very nice, Lila, but you need to blot your lipstick.

Marcelline shows how with a paper napkin. Lila imitates her.

MRS. HEMINGWAY

Ernie should be here any time now. Come along girls. Time to put on our party dresses.

Marcelline and Lila exchange nervous glances. They follow Mrs. Hemingway and Carol to the cottage as Willis appears from the road with flower baskets and boxes. Lila rushes to help him.

LILA
What'd you do? Rob a florist?

WILLIS
A surprise. Mazaween loves fresh flowers.

LILA
What's in the boxes?

WILLIS
Corsages for Carol and the women. A tradition. And this is for you.

LILA
A real rose. I never had a real rose. But I can't.

WILLIS
Why not?

LILA
How do I know you're not...

WILLIS
... playing around, like Ernie down in Cuba? But he's still your hero. I'm just the fool who thinks of your education and tries to help.

LILA
I didn't mean --

WILLIS
-- When you're talking to me, you're talking to him.
(he stops, stunned at what he's said)
Throw away the damned rose.

Willis scoops up the flower boxes and enters the porch.

Lila, dismayed, runs with the rose towards her tent.

EXT. TENT - CONTINUOUS

Lila stops at the driftwood table where her poems still lay.

A moment later, she places the rose on the poems.

The light around the poems and rose turns reddish. It is sunset now.

EXT. LAKE - SUNSET

Lila stares across the lake and admires the beautiful sunset. She hears the nearby partiers. She takes a nervous breath.

EXT. COTTAGE - FRONT YARD - LATER

Marcelline, in a red gown and Spanish shawl, reads to guests clustered around the cards hung on the birthday tree.

MARCELLINE
This birthday card reads: "To Ernie. Farewell to Arms, and legs, and breasts, and..." naughty, naughty.

Guests laugh, applaud.

MARCELLINE (CONT'D)
This one says, "The Sun also Rises. And sets. And rises." It should have been addressed to the "late" Mr. Hemingway. Better get here soon.

Guests mingle and chat as Willis comes from the road and seeks out Lila, who is serving punch.

LILA
Willis, the rose. I apologize.

WILLIS
Soon as you can, meet me at your tent, L.V. It's important.

He joins in singing "Happy Birthday, dear Ernest, wherever you are, happy birthday to you." They blow out candles, applaud.

EXT. LILA'S TENT - NIGHT

Muffled dance music plays in the background. In a patch of moonlight, Willis and Lila face each other.

WILLIS
L.V., I don't know how to tell you, but -- Ernie's still in Cuba. I phoned him just a while ago.

LILA
You lie.

WILLIS
He never intended to come. When his mother phoned, the houseboy misunderstood.

LILA
You lie, you lie. He'll come later.

WILLIS
No, not later. I'm sorry, L.V.

LILA
Every night, every starlit night, every black night since I've been here, I've put down words the way I thought he'd put them down.

Willis reaches to stroke her face but she shoves him away.

LILA (CONT'D)
Every morning, my first thought was -- how would he awake? What would he think? What in the day ahead would he write about?

WILLIS
L.V., don't.

LILA
From the minute I got this job, I walked on sacred ground. And he betrayed me.

Lila rips the ribbon from her birthday folder and throws the poems to the ground where they scatter.

WILLIS
Ernie doesn't even know you exist. How could he betray you?

LILA
I don't know. I don't know anything. I'll never _be_ anything. Not ever.

Willis gathers her poems and they sit together.

WILLIS
I offered to take you down to visit...

Lila gasps -- hopeful.

WILLIS (CONT'D)
... but he's writing. You should understand that. So should Mazaween.

LILA
She wanted to patch up their differences. Says not, but she even bought the Japanese lanterns he loved as a boy.

WILLIS
I hoped she'd show him her play. Get his help to stage it, so she'd be a little famous in her own right.

LILA
(softly)
She and I -- we both needed him.

The dance music ends abruptly, a sign that that the party's over. Ernest has not arrived.

LILA (CONT'D)
Oh, Mrs. Sanford. Poor lamb.

EXT. COTTAGE - FRONT YARD - CONTINUOUS

The guests are embarrassed for Marcelline. They avoid eye contact as they say "Good night," "Delightful," "Wonderful," "Godspeed."

Mrs. Hemingway is with departing guests. She catches Marcelline's eye.

Marcelline slowly shakes her head, disgusted and disapproving. Mrs. Hemingway leans towards Marcelline.

MRS. HEMINGWAY
Don't worry, Mar --

MARCELLINE
-- I'm not.

Marcelline turns her back on her mother and shuffles towards the cottage, her back bent.

Mrs. H looks hurt, but returns to the departing guests.

INT. COTTAGE - LIVING ROOM - LATER

Marcelline, in lamp light in a rocker, has taken a chill. Carol covers her with an afghan as Willis and Lila enter.

Lila starts picking up party debris. Willis kisses the top of Marcelline's head.

MARCELLINE
The flowers were divine. Mother's driving a few guests home. She still thinks Ernie's on his way.

WILLIS
But you know he isn't.

MARCELLINE
The birthday cards are hysterical. The one about "The Sun also..."

WILLIS
I phoned Ernie just a bit ago. He's -- he's still in Cuba.

MARCELLINE
(overlapping)
"... rises and sets, and rises."

WILLIS
Ernie's hard at work on his new novel. His greatest, he says, so he can't come to Walloon, or anywhere, not for a long time.

CAROL
He shouldn't have been invited.

MARCELLINE
(sarcastically)
Another one of mother's dramatic notions.

Her hand comes to her head -- another headache? Lila looks worried.

WILLIS
He's sorry. Truly. He thought it was just one of those "wish you were here" notes from his mother.

MARCELLINE
Don't defend him.

WILLIS
The novel's based on the Spanish Civil War. He's well into it. About sixty thousand words.

Marcelline clutches the rocker arms and rocks faster.

MARCELLINE
We're so different now, Ernie and I. The erstwhile Hemingway twins.

WILLIS
I don't see how your mother thought raising you as twins would work.

MARCELLINE
Oh, but it did.

Marcelline stops rocking and stands. Reaches for the viola.

MARCELLINE (CONT'D)
I got inside Ernie's head. I knew what he thought, what he'd do. I was Ernie. When he was wounded in the war, I was wounded. If he'd died, I'd have died.

She sits in silence for a moment, holding the viola.

She plays a mournful tune on the viola.

SEPIA FLASHBACK - SHORE OF WALLOON LAKE

-- Child Ernest, age 10, raises his rifle and SHOOTS a heron. It falls lifeless to the ground.

MARCELLINE (V.O.) (CONT'D)
When Ernie shot a blue heron and the game warden was after him, he took off in one boat for Horton Bay...

-- Child Marcelline, 11, in overalls, races to an old rowboat, throws in a bundle of boys clothes and a basket of bread and canned beans. She jumps in and rows away in panic.

MARCELLINE (V.O.) (CONT'D)
... And I took off in another boat to bring him food, clothes.

-- Marcelline arrives in her rowboat at Horton Bay. Ernest greets her with a big hug. She looks back nervously to see if she was followed while he grabs the supplies.

He hugs her again, and she jumps back in the boat. Once she is settled, he pushes the boat off.

FROM THE BOAT (SEPIA FLASHBACK CONT'D)

Marcelline looks back at Ernest as he waves at her.

CHILD ERNEST
Thanks, keed.

MARCELLINE (V.O.)
When it was over and nothing bad happened to Ernie...

BACK TO THE COTTAGE LIVING ROOM

MARCELLINE (CONT'D)
... Everyone went on as before -- except me. Even now, I wake at night with a clutch in my stomach, wanting to save my brother.

WILLIS
Oh, Mazaween. I'm so sorry.

Marcelline goes to the window. Her stricken face is reflected in the glass. Lila looks stricken as well.

MARCELLINE
I doted on Ernie. Helped him with his cello. And once, when he had to learn his multiplication tables before he could go on a long fishing trip with Daddy, I drilled Ernie every day for a week. And he went.
(sighs)
He had to learn to eat cold beans from a can, and he did that, too.

Marcelline chuckles, then becomes solemn.

MARCELLINE (CONT'D)
And he learned to make writing bigger than anything, bigger than God, bigger than... family. That's what Ernie can do, and I can't.

WILLIS
Mrs. Hemingway'll be upset.

Lila is caught up in the sadness. She almost kneels in empathy but catches herself.

MARCELLINE
But she'll forgive Ernie. She always docs.
(with bravado)
Well, no use wasting this party stuff. And those lovely Japanese lanterns. Why don't we go down and float them on the lake?

CAROL
(to Lila)
The legend is they carry the spirits of the dead.

WILLIS
Come on, "keeds."
(realizing too late this is Ernie's word)
I've got matches.

EXT. LAKESHORE - LATER

Lila, Carol, Marcelline, and Willis watch as opaque lanterns with lit candles inside float past on the placid lake in the moonlight.

WILLIS
See any dead spirits you know, L.V.?

LILA
No. My mother isn't there. She'll never come to me.

Lila wants to cry, but she holds it in -- L.V.-the-Strong.

LILA (CONT'D)
Neither'll Ernest.

Lila gazes hopelessly at the lanterns on the lake. Willis, affected by her sadness, lays a hand on Lila's shoulder.

Marcelline looks mortally wounded.

The Japanese Lanterns form an eerie funeral procession as they glide down the lake. Marcelline watches them.

MARCELLINE (O.S.)
... Then they drift apart.

The lanterns drift in different directions and nearly out of sight. Marcelline hears muffled crying.

She then notices further down the shore the solitary figure of Mrs. Hemingway. There's such distance between them.

Mrs. H. holds her handkerchief and watches the lanterns disappear. She turns her head and sees Marcelline.

The two forlorn women exchange glances only for a second before Mrs. Hemingway turns away.

FADE TO BLACK.

FADE IN:

EXT. WINDEMERE COTTAGE - DAY

A high wind bends trees as Lila kneels by a hole she has dug. She lifts her folder of birthday poems high, as if for a sacrifice, then buries them and covers the mound with wild asters.

She stands a moment with her red felt hat off in reverence.

She clutches her hat in the wind, races to the canoe at the shore, and shoves off.

EXT. LAKE

The water churns, and Lila paddles furiously. The wind spins her canoe another direction, but she regains direction. Then, her hat blows off.

She paddles towards the hat as white-capped waves slap at the canoe in the deep water and wash inside it.

She manages to grab her red felt hat, but now there is too much water inside the canoe.

LILA

Help! Help!

But her cries are lost in the wind's wail. Frantically, she gets on her knees and uses her hat to bail water.

The canoe tilts and tosses her overboard.

She sinks, then bobs up. She starts to cry help, but a wave fills her mouth. She's choking and thrashing in the waves.

UNDERWATER

Her clothes are heavy. She sinks again. Down. A lake weed wraps around her ankle. She struggles.

She stops just a moment as if she sees something in the distance -- it's another mystical moment.

SEPIA FLASHBACK

Lila is a little girl. Her MOTHER, all comfort and wisdom, hides something behind her back.

Lila stretches out her arms, and her mother gives her a plush deer -- a doe. She hugs the deer, then her mother. It's a hug she needs.

Lila looks straight up at us, as if swimming up towards the ceiling.

ON THE LAKE

Lila surfaces, still struggling.

LILA (CONT'D)

Mama! Mama!

But her arms are tired. She sinks again.

UNDERWATER

From above, a hand reaches down and grabs Lila's. Pulls her up.

ON THE LAKE

Lila sees not her mother, but Willis in his Chris Craft.

He throws her a life preserver, hauls her in. She chokes, spits water and struggles to catch her breath.

Willis wraps her in a blanket, hugs her trembling body close.

He snags the canoe and ties it to his boat, dragging it as he races to

THE SANFORD DOCK

where he ties the canoe to a piling, then walks Lila toward her tent.

EXT. TENT - CONTINUOUS

Lila shivers. Willis puts his arm around her but she shoves him away, angry at herself and embarrassed.

Willis gulps from his flask, offers Lila a sip, but she pushes his hand away.

WILLIS
That was a damned fool thing to do. What if I hadn't come along?

LILA
I'm sorry.

WILLIS
You haven't learned a damned thing. Don't read the sky, the wind. Don't even swim well. Dammit, L.V.

LILA
I almost drowned, and you stand there yelling at me. I'm sorry, I'm sorry, I'm sorry.

WILLIS
You scared the hell out of me. What were you doing at Windemere anyway?

LILA
I buried the poems I wrote for Ernest. That's what you do with dead dreams. You bury 'em.

WILLIS
Maaz'll be upset with you.

LILA
Please don't tell. Please.

WILLIS
You're lucky to be alive.

LILA
I know. When I realized what was happening, I --

Lila suddenly fetches her journal and writes at the table.

LILA (CONT'D)
I have to get it all down, exactly the way the wind buffeted the canoe ... the color of the water... the feel and smell and taste of it... the string of the lake-weed that wrapped around my ankle --

WILLIS
-- So you can write about "The Day I Nearly Drowned"?

LILA
No. So I can write about someone else in a different time, a different place, but the look and feel will be exact. That's what Ernest does.

WILLIS
Know who you remind me of? That poet-painter who buried his poems when the love of his life died. Then, when he had a chance to publish the poems, he dug 'em up.

Lila slaps him playfully with her journal and chases him back to his Chris Craft, her blanket flying.

WILLIS (CONT'D)
What are you waiting for? Write.

Willis guns the boat motor and drives off.

LILA
Wait, wait. I haven't thanked you.

IN THE CHRIS CRAFT

Willis is reflective. He glances back, shakes his head, and holds a fond smile for the tiny figure on the dock.

ON THE DOCK

Lila sits cross-legged and starts writing ferociously in her journal.

EXT. BACK YARD COTTAGE - DAY

In a morning fog, Marcelline sets a picnic basket next to the squeaky water pump. She pumps some water into the dipper.

Marcelline takes the dipper of water to Mrs. Hemingway who walks from the cottage with her easel and paints.

Mrs. Hemingway looks surprised. Marcelline has a loving way about her.

Mrs. Hemingway spots the dipper of water and sets down her paints and easel. She looks completely vulnerable.

MARCELLINE
A drink, Muzz?

MRS. HEMINGWAY
Oh, I love to drink from the dipper.

Her voice falters as she tries to say "Marce."

The dipper plummets to the ground as the two fall in each other's arms.

MRS. HEMINGWAY & MARCELLINE
I'm sorry.

They hold each other.

MARCELLINE
Dear Heart, let's not drift apart.

They smile at each other warmly, both relieved the fighting is over.

MRS. HEMINGWAY
God watches over his little sparrows.
He'll care for us, too.

They kiss each other. Marcelline smiles happily.

MARCELLINE
I made a picnic for you.

EXT. ROADSIDE NEAR THE COTTAGE - CONTINUOUS

Lila sets a broom and pail beside Mrs. H's white Ford, which is oddly parked.

She sees the mailbox flag, finds a letter from Nita, reads it, and gasps.

EXT. COTTAGE - CONTINUOUS

She runs to Marcelline and Mrs. Hemingway, who carry the picnic basket, easel and paints.

MARCELLINE
What is it, Lila? What's wrong?

LILA
Thomas ran away. Had a fight with my father. Why must they fight all the time?

MARCELLINE

Take heart, Lila. When Ernie sent six copies of his first book, Father was shocked at the language and he sent all six copies back. It caused a rift.

Mrs. Hemingway slips her arm around Marcelline.

MRS. HEMINGWAY

... 'Til a few years later, in Key West, his father spotted Ernie fishing on the pier. They fell in each other's arms.

She brushes away tears as her eyes meet Marcelline's.

MRS. HEMINGWAY (CONT'D)

I'm sure your brother's in God's care. Come along.

LILA

I should never have left him.

Marcelline, perhaps identifying with Lila's sisterly fears, clutches Lila.

Softly, "One Fine Day" from Madame Butterfly FADES IN.

MRS. HEMINGWAY

Now, now, come along. You wanted to see my hideaway. And I'll pay you extra to sweep.

Marcelline releases Lila. The three start off together.

Marcelline waves good-bye as Lila climbs into the car.

The opera aria plays in Marcelline's head -- she's humming.

Mrs. Hemingway starts the Ford with an overloud VROOM, VROOM. The car bucks, then fishtails in the gravel and roars off.

But Marcelline is lost in the aria, which is louder now.

SEPIA FLASHBACK - OPERA HOUSE

Teenaged Marcelline and Teenaged Ernest sit together watching Madame Butterfly singing "One Fine Day."

Marcelline has a tear in her eye. She glances up at Ernest, who is obvious touched by the operatic scene.

She leans against Ernest's shoulder. He puts his brotherly arm around her. Tears trickle down their faces.

INT. COTTAGE - MARCELLINE'S DESK AREA - DAY - BACK TO PRESENT DAY

Marcelline still hears the aria. She stares at her typewriter.

EXT. ROAD - CONTINUOUS

Lila watches the woods whiz by her car window. The only sound is the aria.

INT. COTTAGE - CONTINUOUS

Marcelline sits staring at the typewriter. She wants to type. But she can't. The aria continues.

SEPIA FLASHBACK - A KITCHEN

Teenaged Ernest wolfs down oatmeal raisin cookies as quickly as Teenaged Marcelline can flip them off the baking pan.

BACK TO THE COTTAGE

Marcelline taps her finger against her cheek. She has an idea.

EXT. MRS. HEMINGWAY'S HIDEAWAY - DAY

Mrs. Hemingway, in an artist's smock, paints at an easel, and continues singing the same aria (without orchestra).

... And we realize that it has been her voice we've been hearing all along. And it's beautiful.

Lila surveys the spectacular view of the lake from the hilltop. A brown wood shelter peeks from the dense woods.

... But Mrs. Hemingway's painting is of a simple road in the woods from the view of the fork in that road.

Mrs. H's singing segues into humming as she paints. She stops singing with Lila's comment.

LILA
A writer's dream.

MRS. HEMINGWAY
Some women cling to their families, but I must have interludes of peace to compose and commune with God.

Lila strolls through daisy-laden fields where bluebirds swoop and butterflies flutter. She sits on a stump and writes.

LILA
Mrs. Hemingway, I've been wondering -- should I maybe go to a different college? Maybe even... Wellesley?

MRS. HEMINGWAY
You'd have to be wealthy, or have a Sugar Daddy. A man to pay your way in exchange for... favors.
(with a brush stroke)
Remember, Ernie never went to college.

LILA
But he was cultured. I've never been to an opera.

Lila starts to bite her nails, remembers to stop, and writes with fervor, looking up at moments into the sky turning purple and gold.

MRS. HEMINGWAY
I see writing's taken your mind off your brother. Art does that. Oh!
(hands her a bag)
I meant to give you this gift.

From the bag, Lila draws a blue silk dress. She gasps with delight, holds the dress to herself, and pirouettes.

MRS. HEMINGWAY (CONT'D)
Your reward. Your nails look better. And every girl needs a pretty dress to feel beautiful and wear to dances.

LILA
I don't know how to dance.

MRS. HEMINGWAY
Dancing is a joy. And joy is God. So don't be afraid of it.

LILA
I thought Dr. Hemingway said dancing was hell and damnation.

MRS. HEMINGWAY
He was wrong. He even danced at Marce's wedding.

LILA
How can I ever thank you?

MRS. HEMINGWAY
Pay attention to Carol. It's lonely here for a young girl who's shy.

LILA
My writing takes all my time.

MRS. HEMINGWAY
Balance, Lila. Art and love. Balance.

LILA
Carol wants to teach me to dance.
I'll begin with that.

Mrs. Hemingway is pleased.

MRS. HEMINGWAY
I'll pray for your brother, Lila, and
your father. He's a child of God,
too.

LILA
That's what my mother would say. Wish
she could see my pretty new dress.

MRS. HEMINGWAY
She'll come to you when you least expect
it.

LILA
You think so?

MRS. HEMINGWAY
We're often visited by our angel-
mothers. Moments of intuition when
God's thoughts come to us in strange
ways. So keep watch, dear.

EXT. ROADSIDE NEAR THE COTTAGE - LATER

Mrs. Hemingway's car screeches to a halt. The white Ford stops with the front end buried in the bushes.

Instantly, Marcelline and Carol emerge from behind protective trees -- Mrs. H's bad driving is both expected and accepted.

As Lila steps out of the car, Marcelline greets her.

MARCELLINE
Baked you some oatmeal cookies to send
to your brother....

Lila is touched, but only nods and smiles. Marcelline gives her a searching look. Lila looks down.

MARCELLINE (CONT'D)
You all right, Lila?

Lila lifts her head and nods a non-committal "yes."

A worried Marcelline and Carol climb into the car, while Mrs. H remains confidently at the wheel. Marcelline catches Lila's eye and tries to cheer her up.

MARCELLINE (CONT'D)
We'll either be late or dead...

She winks at Lila and nods towards Mrs. H. Lila has to smile.

MARCELLINE (CONT'D)
... But don't worry, okay?

Marcelline is suddenly jerked back in her seat, as the car fish tails out of the brush and bulls down the road.

Lila is alone in the silence. She looks sad and stares off into the woods for a moment... searching.

INT. COTTAGE - SCREENED PORCH - NIGHT

The lantern glows on the dining table as a slow waltz plays on the Victrola. Lila, in her new dress, dances awkwardly in bare feet.

LILA
One-two-three, one-two-three. Oh, darn.

Willis quietly opens the porch door. He wears a blazer, flannels, and a Panama straw hat. In a corner, he props a new fishing rod tied with a bow.

Lila turns and is startled to see him. Before she can speak, he takes her in his arms to dance.

WILLIS
You need a partner. Allow me. One, two, three. One, two -- no, don't wiggle your hips. Glide. Glide.

Lila stumbles but begins to catch on.

WILLIS (CONT'D)
Now, put your head against my shoulder. It's entirely proper. Allows me to lead better. See?

The recording ends but keeps repeating as Willis and Lila sway. Lila pulls away and shuts off the Victrola.

LILA
Dr. Hemingway was right. Dancing leads to hell and damnation.

WILLIS
You're mighty dressed up tonight.

LILA
You, too. I like your hat.

Lila commandeers his Panama hat and puts it on.

LILA (CONT'D)
There. Just what I need. Like it?

Willis laughs and gives her the fishing rod.

LILA (CONT'D)
Oh, Willis. But I can't accept an expensive gift from a man.

WILLIS
Wasn't expensive.

LILA
Was. You left the price tag on.

WILLIS
Damn.

LILA
I know the spot to fish with it. Mrs. Hemingway's hideaway.

WILLIS
How was your day with the Matriarch?

LILA
I want a hideaway like hers on a hill where I can write and commune.

WILLIS
L.V.'s hideaway. Well, stick with me, keed, as Ernie would say.

Willis blows out the lantern. He reaches to embrace Lila but she runs outside. He follows her.

EXT. LAKESHORE IN FRONT OF THE COTTAGE

In the night sky, Northern Lights begin to pulse and flash red, green and white. Lila grabs Willis's arm, alarmed.

LILA
Willis, what's happening up there?

WILLIS
Northern Lights. Storms on the sun spark electricity. Nothing to be scared of.

LILA
They're beautiful. Are they an omen?

WILLIS
Yes. Of good things to come.

Willis spreads his blazer on the ground, and they sit together as the lights play like spotlights at a Hollywood gala.

WILLIS (CONT'D)
Remember I once had the crazy idea I'd like to teach American literature?

LILA
And I said you should have done it.

WILLIS
Could I still?
(clears throat)
Close your eyes. Ready?

Lila closes her eyes and nods "yes."

WILLIS (CONT'D)
My idea is that you and I -- that we -- should go to the University of Michigan -- together.

LILA
(eyes fly open)
You and me? Us? To U of M?

WILLIS
You could get your bachelor's degree and I could get my master's, maybe my doctorate.

LILA
That's crazy. You know it's crazy. You're crazy. How dare you?

Lila leaps up. Willis leaps up, too, and grabs her wrist.

WILLIS
I thought you'd be glad, L.V.

LILA
My, God --

WILLIS
Don't say God.

LILA
God, God, God. You think I should swoon and say, yes, yes, yes.

She turns abruptly.

LILA (CONT'D)
And what would my family think?
(MORE)

LILA (CONT'D)
I have to take care of them, you know. And Mrs. Sanford, Mrs. Hemingway? And me? Going off with a stranger.

WILLIS
And I'm not taking any risks?

LILA
Whatever happened to Wellesley? Or was that just another pipe dream?

WILLIS
Didn't want you that far away.

Willis reaches to hug her. She moves away from him.

LILA
I can't think. If the sky would just stop blinking.

WILLIS
A few minutes ago, you thought the sky was beautiful.

LILA
A few minutes ago, I still had control of my life.

Willis, crestfallen, kicks at the ground.

WILLIS
It was just an idea.

LILA
(tormented)
It's so unfair, 'cause going to the U of M is my secret wish. I can see myself listening to visiting poets. And being published in the literary magazine. And winning the prize.

WILLIS
Then why not?

LILA
Mrs. Sanford said the Americans in Europe are drifting back now, and once your wife comes home...

Willis grasps her hands. They face each other.

WILLIS
I think I love you, L.V.

LILA
... Once she comes home, you'll forget this summer fling. You'll go back to --

She looks hard at him for a moment, thinking.

LILA (CONT'D)
You said, I love you. But maybe you only meant, I'm crazy about you.

Lila pulls her hand away.

LILA (CONT'D)
I just don't want a Sugar Daddy. I'll pay for my own education.

WILLIS
Sugar Daddy? Where'd you get that vulgar idea? I'm ready to sacrifice everything for you, and you insult me?

LILA
I'm upset. I've made promises to myself, to Mrs. Sanford.

Lila bites her nails, then throws them behind her back.

LILA (CONT'D)
And I can't desert Thomas. He ran away. Might again.

WILLIS
I could make a suggestion about Thomas, but I'm a Sugar Daddy.

LILA
What about Thomas?

Willis lifts her chin with one hand and looks in her eyes.

WILLIS
Why not have Thomas live with us? He could have his own apartment in our house.

LILA
. Our house?

Willis smiles. Hopeful.

WILLIS
I'll find a nice little house near the campus. Send him to a private day school. Summers, I'll have my son, too. Teach both boys to hunt and fish.

Lila puts her arms around his neck.

LILA
Would you do that? For Thomas and me?

WILLIS
I'd do anything for you, L.V. We'll be orphan twins, you and I, and live like the Hemingways.

They embrace tenderly.

LILA
Give my baby sister ballet lessons.

WILLIS
Go to concerts and plays.

LILA
To the opera.

WILLIS
You go to the opera.

LILA
I'll have my hideaway.

WILLIS
And we'll fly with the loons. I'll teach you.

LILA
How I want to fly....

He takes off her Panama hat. They kiss passionately.

LILA (CONT'D)
In "A Farewell to Arms," Catherine wants Frederic so much she wants to be Frederic.

WILLIS
I want to be you, too, Catherine. Here. Now.

Willis puts the Panama hat back on her head and steers her toward her tent. The Northern Lights fade.

Willis holds open the tent flap to enter.

Lila panics. She pushes him away. Startled, he stares, disbelieving.

LILA
No, no. Ernie's tent is... holy -- and I -- No -- And...

Willis drops the tent flap. Angry and frustrated, he strides to the dock, leaps into his boat.

LILA (CONT'D)
... And if Mrs. Sanford....

He looks back at her hopefully, but she is still shocked, frozen. So he roars off.

The distant sound of the Chris Craft gives way to silence. Lila stares out at the black lake. Alone.

A plaintive viola solo plays.

SEPIA FLASHBACK - WINDEMERE

Ernest -- looking very much like Willis only without the mustache -- wears his World War I uniform. He walks with great effort, using crutches.

Young Marcelline carries a bucket of water towards the cottage, but when she sees Ernest, she drops the bucket in alarm, grabs her stomach as if wounded, and rushes to him.

INSIDE WINDEMERE COTTAGE (SEPIA FLASHBACK CONT'D)

Ernest lies on a bed hugging his Red Cross afghan, being brave as Marcelline attends to the shrapnel-caused fluids oozing from his legs.

Marcelline stops a moment to look at Ernest's devil-may-care expression while he continues to hug the Red Cross afghan. She smiles and touches his hair.

ERNEST
I don't know who's worse off -- the Old Brute or...
(having fun)
... Mazaween.

He chuckles. The viola music suddenly stops.

INT. COTTAGE - LIVING ROOM - CONTINUOUS

Marcelline looks downward as if looking at Ernest, the viola bow in her hand. She's still with her memory.

MARCELLINE
I worry about you.

Marcelline awakes from her memory. She's in a silk dress, straw hat, pearls, and pumps; and sits in a straight chair.

She resumes playing the viola, only this time a romantic sonata. An overnight bag and white gloves rest on the floor at her feet.

Lila, still forlorn, has nonetheless dressed up in shorts and shirt, fixed her hair, and wears light lipstick. She hovers.

Marcelline continues to play as she gives instructions.

MARCELLINE (CONT'D)
I left a note in the kitchen, the address where we'll stay overnight. At the reception after the concert, Mother and Carol'll meet my buddies from my Chautauqua days.

LILA
(softly)
Imagine.

MARCELLINE
Imagine.

The music swells. Marcelline, enraptured, tilts her head.

MARCELLINE (CONT'D)
It brings back the summer I played with the Bay View Orchestra.

Marcelline's smile and far-away gaze show she is transported to the halcyon summer of concerts in the park.

SEPIA FLASHBACK - A GAZEBO IN A PARK IN SUMMER, 1917

Teenaged Marcelline, 19, continues playing the same sonata on the viola, but is joined by several musicians. Their music floats on the night air.

A BANNER on the gazebo says "BAY VIEW CHAUTAUQUA"

PRE-LAP - A car horn BLARES.

BACK IN COTTAGE LIVING ROOM

Marcelline startles. Mrs. Hemingway BEEPS the car horn from the road.

MARCELLINE (CONT'D)
Coming! Take care, Lila.

Marcelline rushes to the road with her overnight bag.

Lila, looking forlorn, strolls to

EXT. WOODED GLEN - DAY

where she searches for tufts of deer fur. Twigs snap, leaves rustle. Sounds of hoofprints come from her tent yard.

LILA
(whispers softly)
A deer?

She tiptoes, hoping to surprise a deer as she draws closer to the sounds. She bends, looking for hoofprints

EXT. LILA'S TENT - CONTINUOUS

where the rustling is louder. She looks up, startled, and finds that the deer is actually Willis. She is stunned.

LILA
Oh, darn. I thought you were a deer.

WILLIS
Well, don't look so disappointed.

Lila beats on his chest. He laughs, grabs her hands.

WILLIS (CONT'D)
I've got the picnic, the fishing rods, the boat. Let's go.

Lila sees the dreamcatcher spinning in the sun, but she looks uncertain.

WILLIS (CONT'D)
Please, Catherine. Just one day. One glorious day.

LILA
Yes, Frederic. One day.

Lila takes the Panama hat hanging on a limb and puts it on. The pair, holding hands, run to the boat.

EXT. SECLUDED SHORE - LATER

Lila and Willis cast from the shore into the lily pads. Lila starts to speak, but Willis hushes her.

They both reel in and cast again. Suddenly a bass THRASHES on Lila's line. Her rod bends. Willis leans over, nets the fish. Lila holds it up.

LILA
Oh, you beautiful bass. I love you.

WILLIS
Now you have to gut it and fry it.

LILA
(unconvincingly)
I'm game.

EXT. LAKE BEACH - LATER

Lila, looking up, refuses to look down at the bass.

WILLIS
Now just scrape the entrails out with your fingers.

We only see her facial reactions -- always looking up -- as she guts the fish.

WILLIS (CONT'D)
That's it.

Lila notices her whippoorwill in the sky. Her face relaxes and she smiles. Lila makes the sound.

LILA
Whip-poor-will. Whip-poor-will

EXT. ANOTHER BEACH SHORE AMID LILY PADS - LATER

The whippoorwill flies off. Lila follows its movement.

She looks down -- she is kneeling and holding a frying pan over a campfire. Willis leans over and nuzzles her.

LILA
Stop that. If I burn this fish, it could ruin our future. Who'd want a woman who can't fry the fish?

WILLIS
Try me.

Willis pulls her back toward him. Her hat falls off. The frying pan falls into the fire. Lila and Willis untangle themselves.

Willis, on one elbow, stretches beside her and traces her face. Lila traces his face. Their eyes close as they kiss without restraint.

Gulls flutter over them, then fly away over the lake.

EXT. A COUNTRY AIRFIELD - NIGHT

Under a full moon, Lila and Willis run to his Piper Cub in a pasture. A wind sock hangs limp near a shed. Willis holds open the passenger door for Lila.

WILLIS
I bought this baby just for you, so we could chase the moon on a night like this -- and you could write a poem about it.

Willis boosts Lila inside and climbs in on the pilot's side.

The motor SPUTTERS, CATCHES, then ROARS as the plane wavers down the pasture and takes off in a steep climb.

INT. PIPER CUB (FLYING) - CONTINUOUS

Lila and Willis fly in silvery moonlight amid a myriad of stars. Willis puts his hand on her knee; she puts it back on the plane's controls but leans affectionately against him.

WILLIS
The house lights look like fireflies.

LILA
That one's our new summer home. And that one's my hideaway with a candle in the window.

WILLIS
And you writing poems when you should come home to me and the children.

Willis puts his hand on her knee again. This time she doesn't remove it and soon he is stroking her thigh. They gaze at the luminous moon.

LILA
Like a balloon on a string, just out of reach.

Willis turns to kiss her and the plane nose dives, tilting them forward. Both his hands are at the controls now. Lila gasps.

He regains control. Lila laughs, relieving tension.

LILA (CONT'D)
Oh, Willis. As long as I live, I'll never forget you and me chasing the moon.

She gazes at the moon's reflection on the lake, highlighting the ripples on the water.

EXT. LAKE - CONTINUOUS

The motor CUTS OUT, the plane wobbles and begins to descend.

INT. PIPER CUB

Lila turns to Willis who is petrified.

She nearly panics and grabs his arm, but he shakes her off. He focuses.

EXT. PASTURE

The piper wobbles, descending for a landing... or a crash.

INT. PIPER CUB

Willis re-starts the motor, but it fails again -- sputtering.

Lila wrings her hands. Looks around and sees nothing but trees all around. She shudders.

EXT. PASTURE

The piper touches down, sudden and hard.

Lila, a loud, truncated gasp.

The plane bounces along the pasture.

Just as quickly, a wing tip grazes a tree -- CRACK! -- and spins the plane.

INT. PIPER CUB

Lila screams as trees spin past her. She bumps her head and is momentarily dazed.

After coming to a stop, Willis hugs Lila to him until she rouses.

WILLIS
Oh, Lila. Lila.

EXT. PIPER CUB

Willis jumps to the ground, runs to the passenger side and helps Lila to the ground.

They stand, solemn and shaken. He touches a tiny bruise on her forehead. And as he does, she gazes at the moon.

LILA
Ouch. That's tender.

WILLIS
I'm sorry, L.V. So sorry.

LILA
Bet the moon was startled, being chased by two crazy people.

WILLIS
Crazy. Deliriously crazy. Oh, God.

LILA
Don't say God.

They laugh in relief as they step away from the plane.

EXT. PASTURE - CONTINUOUS

They walk arm-in-arm to his convertible.

LILA
When you come back on Labor Day, we need to make plans.

WILLIS
You'll miss the chance to march in the Labor Day parade... and sing "Solidarity Forever."

LILA
Does that make you happy?

They stop at his convertible.

WILLIS
I like the rebel in you.

Willis takes a card from his jacket pocket.

WILLIS (CONT'D)
Here's my post office box. Write me there... and no tears.

LILA
No tears. When you get to U of M, Frederic, send a postcard with "X" marks the English Building.

WILLIS
And send me your poems, Catherine.

Their emotions spent, they embrace sweetly, childlike.

LILA
May we have many full moons.

They pull back and stare as if memorizing each other's faces.

And gulls fly pass the moon, which is still in the sky.

FADE TO BLACK.

FADE IN:

EXT. HORTON BAY GENERAL STORE - DAY

A bell jingles as Marcelline, Lila, and Mrs. Hemingway enter an old-fashioned white, wooden store with a false, two-story front.

The sign says: "Horton Bay General Store, 1876."

INT. HORTON BAY GENERAL STORE

They wander narrow aisles crammed with supplies. The tin ceiling is hung with old lanterns, tools.

Suddenly Lila bolts from the store, Marcelline following, and runs down the dirt road to the

HORTON BAY SHORE

where she bursts from the road and stands at the water's edge near a sawdust heap and a limestone chunk adjacent to an old lumber mill. Sadly, she shades her eyes as if looking for a boat.

Marcelline, breathless, appears and sits on the limestone, gulping for air. Lila explains.

LILA
I wanted to see where Ernest's story takes place, the one where Nick Adams breaks up with his girlfriend. Ernest called it "The End of Something."

MARCELLINE
As I remember, Nick was cruel. He said love wasn't fun anymore.

LILA
And she loved him so much. Loved being with him, fishing with him. And she was so dignified. She just got in the boat and rowed off.
(shaking her head)
I don't think I could bear it....

Marcelline shoots her a knowing look.

MARCELLINE
It's the risk you take. Like walking a tightrope over Niagra Falls. If you should tumble for the wrong man...

Marcelline rises and starts back to the store.

Lila follows, head bowed, glimpsing in her mind for the first time a serpent in her new-found paradise.

INT. COTTAGE - NIGHT

Marcelline, Carol, and Mrs. Hemingway march through the cottage singing the "Song of the Toreador" only with new lyrics:

THE THREE
Toreador-a/ don't spit on the floor-a/
Use the cuspidor-a/ That's what it's
for-a.

Suddenly, Marcelline spots something through the window.

EXT. COTTAGE - CONTINUOUS

A male figure moves stealthily through the darkness, but away from the cottage.

INT. COTTAGE - CONTINUOUS

Marcelline touches her heart -- startled, afraid.

INT. TENT - CONTINUOUS

Lila writes in her journal by lantern light.

She hears something outside -- is it the deer?

She sees a hand slide through the tent flap. She prepares to scream.

At once, the scared face of Thomas, her teenaged kid brother, pokes through the flap. Lila looks curious, dumbfounded.

LILA
Thomas?

That's enough to encourage him in. They hug each other, then Thomas talks fast, relieved that he's found Lila.

THOMAS
It's laid out just like you said in
your letter. The cottage over there --

LILA
-- What?

She seems to notice for the first time the bruises on Thomas's face, and how scared he is. He notices and explains.

THOMAS
The cops is after me. I --

EXT. TENT

Marcelline is there -- eavesdropping.

LILA (O.S.)
-- Listen. If you did something bad,
tell me now, so when --

Marcelline softens as she listens to Thomas.

THOMAS (O.S.)
I didn't -- well, I ran away -- but on my way here some men 'spected me of something and hit me. I got away, but they called the cops.

Marcelline moves towards the tent flap.

SEPIA FLASHBACK - THE TENT

Marcelline opens the tent flap.

Teenaged Ernest is in the tent, quickly gathering supplies. He looks a bit scared, but hides it when he sees Teenaged Marcelline. The same lantern is lit.

TEENAGED MARCELLINE
Ernie, if you did something bad --

TEENAGED ERNEST
That heron I shot? Well, now the warden wants me --

TEENAGED MARCELLINE
You deserve whatever you got coming.

She gazes at him a moment and softens.

TEENAGED ERNEST
(bravado)
I know where to hide.

Marcelline is resigned. She shakes her head.

TEENAGED MARCELLINE
You and me against the world.

BACK TO LILA AND THOMAS INSIDE THE TENT

Lila listens carefully to her brother's story.

THOMAS
... Daddy always yellin' -- saying I'm no good. An' if Nita sticks up for me, he fights with her. And then the baby cries, an' <u>you're</u> not there.

OUTSIDE THE TENT

Marcelline looks like she might cry.

LILA (O.S.)
And so you ran.

INSIDE THE TENT

THOMAS
Just like you. You ran away to here, didn't you?

LILA
(suddenly stricken)
Yes, I ran away.

They collapse into an embrace.

LILA (CONT'D)
I missed you -- you little brat.

OUTSIDE THE TENT

Lila's statement resonates a deep, painful chord in Marcelline.

INSIDE THE TENT

THOMAS
I'm scared, Sis. What do we do?

LILA
Well, you can't stay here.

Suddenly, Marcelline steps into the tent.

Both Thomas and Lila SCREAM in fright until Lila recognizes Marcelline.

MARCELLINE
I know where to hide.

Lila and Thomas are stunned.

LILA
What?

MARCELLINE
... Until I can get Ernie a bus ticket back.

LILA
Ernie? You mean Thomas? But we can't afford --

MARCELLINE
-- Don't worry about it. But you should call home and tell them your brother's safe. And coming home.

THOMAS
I ain't going back. He'll rave.

LILA
(to Thomas)
You've gotta go back 'cause you've...

LILA & THOMAS
... Gotta go to college

Thomas laughs briefly.

LILA
Don't worry, I'll talk to dad.

THOMAS
... Just like always...

LILA
... It's you and me against the world.

Lila looks up at Marcelline, whose eyes are misty.

LILA (CONT'D)
You are so kind, Mrs. Sanford. So very kind.

Marcelline is so choked up, she can hardly speak.

MARCELLINE
You're his big sister.

CUT TO

EXT. BUS STOP - DAY

Thomas leans out the bus window. He waves to Lila, who stands with Marcelline.

Marcelline looks melancholy as she watches the bus pull out.

SEPIA FLASHBACK - TRAIN STATION

Teenaged Ernest, 19, leans out the train window in his World War I Red Cross uniform. He waves to Marcelline.

She watches the train chug away.

BACK AT THE BUS STOP

Lila watches the bus drive away.

LILA
He is so kind at heart, and I didn't even leave him a good-bye note when I left for Walloon.

Marcelline puts an arm around Lila.

MARCELLINE
I know. I forgot to thank Ernie for the names of people to see in Paris. And other times he was kind. Many times.

They start walking down the road together, like twins.

MARCELLINE (CONT'D)
Mother's life'd be quite different if Ernie hadn't set up a trust fund for her after Daddy died. I'd forgotten that, too.

Marcelline looks weary. Holds her head -- headache.

LILA
Let's hurry back. I'll make tea sandwiches so you can work on your play.

MARCELLINE
I -- I suddenly feel suffocated by too many memories.
(sighs)
Or maybe it's all the war talk. The radio said Germany's sending U-boats to thc North Atlantic.

LILA
If... when... war comes, I'll join the Red Cross, like Ernest.

Marcelline stops. Holds Lila's shoulders. She's serious.

MARCELLINE
Before you take care of soldiers, take care of yourself. Be wise.

FADE TO BLACK.

FADE IN:

EXT. COTTAGE FRONT YARD - LABOR DAY

Yellow, red leaves twirl down, the first signs of autumn.

Carol and Lila pare apples at the picnic table. Lila wears her blue silk dress under her apron, new shoes, and her Panama hat.

A letter for Marcelline is on the table. Popular music BLARES from the radio on the steps.

CAROL
When Willis gets here today for the Labor Day shindig, show him how you can jitterbug.

LILA
That's our little secret.

CAROL
Mom's afraid you're going to get hurt.

Lila nicks her finger and sucks it.

LILA
Darn, darn.
(wielding her bloody finger)
Want some.

CAROL
You're funny.

Marcelline and Mrs. Hemingway stroll from the cottage. Carol runs to Marcelline with the letter.

CAROL (CONT'D)
For you, Mother. From the Detroit Motion Picture Council.

MARCELLINE
Oh, mercy.
(opens the letter)
It says "to represent the American Association of University Women, to preview all new films." -- And I'll see them free!

Marcelline glances at Mrs. Hemingway, who looks dour.

MARCELLINE (CONT'D)
Muzz, aren't you glad for me?

MRS. HEMINGWAY
It's just that movies are so sensual.

MARCELLINE
(teasing)
Compared to opera? To Don Giovanni, that lecher? Really, Mother.

CAROL
Wait 'til I tell the kids at school. You'll see Gone With the Wind first.

The music on the radio STOPS -- there is static -- and then British Prime Minister NEVILLE CHAMBERLAIN's voice comes through the radio. But he can't be heard over Marcelline.

MARCELLINE
Come along, Carol, Mustn't miss the boat parade. Your brothers built a raft --

Marcelline stops. Everyone is instantly silent. Motionless.

CHAMBERLAIN (V.O.)
...a state of war would exist between us. I have to tell you now that... [static] ... and that consequently this country is at war with Germany.

Lila runs to the radio, leans close. STATIC blots out the news. Lila CLICKS it off.

LILA
It's happened.

Marcelline and Mrs. Hemingway bow their heads.

MRS. HEMINGWAY
I prayed there'd never be another war.

Boat horns sound from the lake.

CAROL
Mama, we'll miss the parade.

EXT. SANFORD DOCK - DAY

Carol and Mrs. Hemingway wait in the rowboat. Marcelline turns to Lila, can't find words and simply squeezes her hand, then climbs into the boat and they shove off.

Lila removes her apron and hurries toward the cottage.

EXT. COTTAGE - BACK YARD

She slips into the hammock where she rocks herself furiously with her straw hat lying on her chest. Eyes closed, she bites her lips to stem the tears as...

... Willis strolls in from the road. He has shaved his moustache and wears a replica of Ernest's World War I uniform, with cane.

Willis hovers above Lila, who opens her eyes. She sees what appears to be a vision of young Ernest Hemingway.

Speechless, she falls out of the hammock. She looks again.

LILA
You look like the ghost of --

WILLIS
-- young Ernie? Home from the last war? He was a handsome devil. Aren't I handsome?

Willis spreads the cape to pose, then helps Lila up. She sits in the hammock. Willis rocks it, so she lays down.

LILA
You look... interesting with no moustache and in that uniform. Where...?

WILLIS
Got it from an old actor buddy for Mazaween's play. A professor at the U of M's going to produce it.

LILA
She'll be thrilled.
(drops her gaze)
But you didn't write. Not even a postcard. I waited and waited. I began to think --

WILLIS
-- I tried to write, but I couldn't.
(looking guilty)
Don't sulk. I'm sorry.

LILA
Did you get my poems? Were they overwritten?

WILLIS
Just a tiny bit.

Willis suddenly dumps the hammock. Lila squeals. Her hat rolls away.

Willis, laughing, doesn't help her to her feet, recapturing their early playfulness.

Lila stands and brushes herself off. Willis turns solemn.

WILLIS (CONT'D)
Are we alone?

Lila nods yes. Willis embraces her with ardor.

WILLIS (CONT'D)
I've missed you, L.V. You'll never know how much.

Lila picks up her hat and abruptly strides past her tent. Willis, bewildered, walks beside her. They enter

THE WOODED GLEN

where they pass through shafts of slanting sunlight amid the greens, golds, and reds of the trees.

WILLIS (CONT'D)
Stop, Lila. I have other news. I was accepted at U of M in the master's program. Someone dropped out. I start in a few weeks.

LILA
(stunned)
I -- I'm glad. If you had to wait a year, we might be at war.

They resume walking.

WILLIS
I heard about England and France on the car radio.

LILA
War makes everything else seem vain.

Willis grabs Lila's arm to halt her, and tilts her chin.

WILLIS
Smile, L.V. Look at you. Look how you've changed. You're not the girl who wanted Ernie to discover her and make love to her.

LILA
Never wanted him to make love.

WILLIS
You did. I found it charming.

Lila pulls away and runs to the matted ferns.

LILA
Willis, this is the place where my ghost deer lives. I wish the deer were here now -- to help me.

WILLIS
Help you?

LILA
Dear heart, turn your back and I'll turn mine. Catherine has something important to tell you.

Lila turns his shoulders, then turns herself so they stand back to back. Her voice quavers at first.

LILA (CONT'D)
About our little house near the campus, it became very real to me. I inhabited every room. I saw the sun filter in through the curtains in summer. I felt the chill of autumn evenings. I watched you light a fire on the hearth in winter.

WILLIS
L.V., don't.

LILA
I grew to love that little house, as I grew to love you. But I'll never live there.
(clears her throat)
I'm not going with you. Not to U of M. Not anywhere. Now now. Not ever.

WILLIS
Oh, L.V.

Lila's eyes are pained.

LILA
I want you to go home and take care of your family -- your little boy who speaks French -- and I'm going home to take care of mine.
(determined)
One way or another, I'll finish college. And one way or another, I'll write. I just don't know how... without you.

Lila and Willis turn to face each other. A breeze frees a few leaves that flutter around.

LILA (CONT'D)
Say good-bye to Catherine.

WILLIS
Good-bye, Catherine.

LILA
Good-bye, Frederic.

Loons cry as they fly high over the swaying trees and the tiny figures below.

EXT. COTTAGE - FRONT YARD - DAY

Marcelline, Carol and Mrs. Hemingway come ashore from the rowboat and start walking to the cottage.

Willis and Lila emerge from the woods and walk toward them.

Mrs. Hemingway stops when she sees Willis. Tears suddenly flow, and she throws open her arms. She embraces Willis before he can speak.

MRS. HEMINGWAY
Ernest... dear boy. Ernest.

Mrs. Hemingway goes limp. Carol and Marcelline each take an arm and assist her to a lawn chair.

MARCELLINE
Willis? What on earth?

Mrs. Hemingway is momentarily confused.

WILLIS
Good news, Maaz. U of M wants to produce your play.
(to Mrs. H.)
I had this costume made so I can play Ernie.

MRS. HEMINGWAY
You frightened me, Willis. Brought back... the...

Marcelline takes a few steps to a nearby willow and hugs it.

MARCELLINE
... The heartache.

It's weeping branches fall over her face like a veil.

MARCELLINE (CONT'D)
Once Ernie told me not to be afraid to taste all the other things in life -- that there's a big world out there where people live and love and die with all their feelings. I wondered then if Ernie would ever again be happy at home.

Marcelline, in tears and anger, walks up to Willis.

MARCELLINE (CONT'D)
And you dare dress up like him?

WILLIS
I'm sorry, Mazaween.

MARCELLINE
My name's Marcelline, remember?
(recovering her poise)
It's nice about my play, Willis, but --

WILLIS
-- I only meant to give you a little fame, too, like your brother's.

MARCELLINE
Suddenly, I'm not interested in a little fame like my brother's. The price....

WILLIS
I'm sorry.

Marcelline stares for a long moment at Lila, then steps closer to Willis and braces herself for what she is about to say.

MARCELLINE
I'm glad everything worked out so beautifully for you and Bonnie.

WILLIS
Yes.

Lila steps back, alarmed. She watches wide-eyed.

MARCELLINE
Bonnie's note came yesterday. She said since you met her boat in New York, she's walked on air. She's thrilled you're going back to U of M.

Lila throws her hands to her mouth to suppress a cry. Willis fidgets -- on the hot seat.

WILLIS
Yes. Touche again.

Marcelline, seeing Willis's distress, continues to taunt him and open Lila's eyes.

MARCELLINE
She's found a nice little house for all of you near the campus. For a second honeymoon, she says.

WILLIS
We want you to visit when we're settled. Maybe when they produce your play. See you then.

Willis turns to go. Lila grabs his sleeve as he passes. Marcelline observes painfully.

LILA
You knew. All the while you knew, and didn't tell me. You let me go on about how I --

WILLIS
-- I wanted to spare you.

LILA
It hurt so much to send you away 'cause you awakened a sweet part of me.

WILLIS
L.V., I --

Willis turns to Marcelline for help, but her disapproving stance tells him he's in deep tapioca. He turns back to Lila.

WILLIS (CONT'D)
Because I'm not Ernie.
(he lets that sink in)
Never was. I don't have his talent -- or his gallantry. He left his wife and child to marry the woman he....
(touching her face)
Well... I couldn't.

The pain deepens in Lila's eyes.

WILLIS (CONT'D)
When I saw my wife and my little boy on the dock in New York --

LILA
Then... chasing the moon was a lie? You knew, even then.

WILLIS
I turned back a dozen times that day before I came to get you. But as Ernie might say, the things that happen to us aren't always things we can control.

He wheels and walks to the road, turns back.

WILLIS (CONT'D)
I'm sorry.

Willis, the Ernest Hemingway "twin," hurries out of sight.

Lila holds out her arms to Mrs. Hemingway, Marcelline and Carol, then slides, face forward, to the ground. She gives a high, thin WAIL, and breaks into muffled weeping.

CAROL
Mother, do something. Lila's crying. Stop her from crying.

MARCELLINE
No. Lila has needed to cry for a very, very long time.

Marcelline kneels beside Lila and gently strokes her hair.

EXT. WALLOON LAKE - DAY

Beautiful fall foliage. In TIME LAPSE, the sun sets and creates a wondrous sunset, which darkens into night. The starry sky is clean and beautiful.

MONTAGE - LILA MOURNS HER LOST LOVE

-- At night at the airfield, she looks at the scarred tree where the wing hit. Finds fragments of the wing tip.

-- At the same airfield, she tosses a white balloon on a string into the air, and watches as the balloon floats up in the moonlight and disappears.

-- In the early morning, Lila walks the shore. She gazes at the beautiful trees, into the woods....

-- Lila stands at the shore where she caught the bass, and takes off her Panama hat. She sails it into the lily pads where it bobs, then tilts and sinks.

-- Lila strolls mournfully in the wooded glen, and bends over the silky heads of milkweeds gone to seed. The sun floods the woods with golden light.

As she straightens, she looks directly into the face of the deer -- harmless, wise, mystical -- exposing its flank, its head turned facing Lila.

They freeze.

Lila is hypnotized as she stares into the marble-like, brown eyes of the deer.

They stand transfixed. A mystical connection.

Lila has the expression of someone comforted beyond measure.

Then the deer leaps away, its tail like a flag.

Lila gasps, starts to chase the deer, then halts as it disappears. She places her hand over her heart, a beatific expression on her face.

FADE TO BLACK.

FADE IN:

EXT. LILA'S TENT - DAY

Another dawn. Golden light. Loons cry overhead.

Lila looks very much a mature young woman, wearing a stylish sweater, plaid skirt, and beret. Her suitcase sits nearby.

She removes the last pole of her nearly deflated tent that SHUSHES in a heap.

Lila kneels, gathers a corner in her arms, and rocks with it like a mother holding a child, as...

... Marcelline appears in her wool robe, carrying a gift-wrapped package. Lila looks up, sees Marcelline, and explains.

LILA
I'm saying farewell -- to my cocoon.

MARCELLINE
Your cocoon?

LILA
I'll never hear the rain but I'll hear the muffled thunk-thunk against canvas. And I'll remember sweating on hot days and shivering on cold nights -- the smell of mold, the scent of pine, and writing by lantern light.

MARCELLINE
I told you, Walloon's enchanted.

Marcelline holds out her gift package. Lila unwraps Ernest's lantern, gasps, and holds it aloft.

MARCELLINE (CONT'D)
It's a talisman. To help you write the next Great American Novel.

LILA
Oh, my... gosh!

Lila hangs the lantern on the nail in the pine tree and sits beside Marcelline.

LILA (CONT'D)
You come to my autographing and I'll come to your opening night.

MARCELLINE
I've given up my Hemingway play. It keeps me in the past.

LILA
But your writing?

MARCELLINE
I'll always write. I may even put the Hemingways in a book some day. But meanwhile, I have my Sterling, and the children. And mother.

LILA
You write so well, do so many things well...

MARCELLINE
... and try too hard to live up to my idols -- my mother, my brother.
(nodding affirmatively)
What I need is to be myself.

Marcelline and Lila rise and stroll toward the road, Lila dragging the tent behind her.

LILA
Sometimes I think we're alike -- I mean, at least, in some ways --

MARCELLINE
(joking)
Like twins, maybe.

LILA & MARCELLINE
Imagine.

They both laugh.

EXT. COTTAGE - BACK YARD

Lila, grunting, rolls and pushes the tent into the shed. Shuts the door. Looks at Marcelline.

LILA
You look more relaxed, Mrs. Sanford.

MARCELLINE
Giving up the play leaves me free to enjoy the moment.
(sighs)
When the war comes, I'm afraid there won't be time for simple pleasures, like the beauty of this dawn...

LILA
... with the sun so pale, the sky so high, as if a lid opened, then another lid 'til there's no end to the height, the blueness.

They stroll across the yard.

MARCELLINE
This will seem like a dream, Lila, when you're back in school. When you're working on the college paper.

Marcelline smiles and puts her arm around Lila.

LILA
If only I didn't still worry about my brother.

MARCELLINE
You'll always worry about your brother.

Mrs. Hemingway and Carol enter the yard carrying bundles.

MARCELLINE (CONT'D)
Good thing you packed the car last night, Muzz. Hate to see you go.

MRS. HEMINGWAY
Carol, you help your Mother when we're gone. And Lila, no chatter in the car. Had to train Marce not to say "Look out, look out." God directs me on the road. That's sufficient.

Marcelline and Lila exchange knowing smiles and shrugs. All start to the road except Lila.

LILA
Wait, everyone. I have a farewell poem to read to you.

Lila opens her journal as the group gathers around her.

LILA (CONT'D)
Last night, it came to me. Ernest never said the things he wanted to say. His story called "The Big Two-Hearted River" was about coming home from the war, but it doesn't have a single word about the war. That's what I have to do, so I wrote this poem.

She gazes momentarily at Marcelline.

LILA (CONT'D)
It seems to be about the deer I saw in the woods....

Marcelline places her hand over her heart.

Mrs. Hemingway clutches her handkerchief.

They know about the deer.

FLASHBACK - LILA'S DEER - harmless, wise, and mystical.

LILA (V.O.) (CONT'D)
It's called "Visitation," by L.V. Nobis.

BACK TO SCENE

Lila clears her throat.

LILA (CONT'D)
You patrol the forest, head held high, gliding through underbrush clean as the moon.

Lila lifts her chin confidently.

LILA (CONT'D)
I track you, look for bruised leaves, snagged fur, footprints arrowed in sand. Just as I despair, you appear, a wall of brown-gray hide, so close I see a twig stuck in your flank. You see all my bones. We are fused.

Lila pauses. A memory. It touches her deeply.

LILA (CONT'D)
You ease my ache, then you are gone.
(a heartfelt sigh)
Now your shadow passes as in a dream, comforting me.

All stand transfixed, stunned by the beauty of the incident.

Mrs. Hemingway nods knowingly. She catches Lila's eye.

MRS. HEMINGWAY
The deer -- the visitation -- somehow, it was your mother.

Lila's chin quivers.

LILA
Yes, a comfort. My Mother-spirit.

Again, everyone is silent.

Marcelline embraces Lila, who smiles joyfully.

CAROL
Will you ever write about us, Lila?

LILA
Some day. Just like "Green Hills of Africa..." they're afraid at the end they won't remember J.P.'s face. But Ernest tells them he'll remember....

Lila hugs her journal.

LILA (CONT'D)
... That's what we do when we write. We remember... and we put people in.

Marcelline closes her eyes and smiles wistfully.

MARCELLINE
Yes. We remember.

MRS. HEMINGWAY
Mercy, better hurry, or we'll hit big city traffic. Come along, Lila.

The three Hemingway generations (plus Lila) start down the road towards the poorly parked Ford.

Suddenly, Lila bolts back down the road.

EXT. CLEARING NEAR THE COTTAGE - CONTINUOUS

The grass is matted where the tent once stood. Ernie's lantern hangs from the nail in the pine tree. Lila's hand grabs it.

Lila holds the lantern high and twirls slowly in a circle like a priest blessing the place.

LILA (V.O.)
When I returned to college, I kept that summer private 'cause if I said I had gone in search of Ernest Hemingway, they'd have seen the silly girl I was.

SEPIA FLASHBACK - THE WALLOON SHORE

Child Ernest Hemingway, age 5, wears an overlarge straw hat and carries a fishing pole over his shoulder like a proud soldier carrying a rifle.

He stops and smiles right at us.

LILA (V.O.) (CONT'D)
They would not have seen that in some strange way, I found him -- in the woods, at the shore, in the bass that thrashed in the lily pads.

DISSOLVE TO:

EXT. WALLOON LAKE - DAY

Loons among lily pads lift themselves into the sky and yodel as they swoop over the Sanford cottage, then dip over Windemere, the ghostly boarded-up summer home Ernest never visited that summer or ever after.

The loons soar above the lake and autumn woods.

LILA (V.O.)
And I found his truth -- that life isn't simple. That pain comes with love.

DISSOLVE TO:

EXT. CLEARING NEAR THE COTTAGE - CONTINUOUS

Near where the tent once stood, the whippoorwill perches on the now-familiar bough of the pine tree.

LILA (V.O.)
And I found my own place, my own people, my own voice.

Lila lifts her gaze to the whippoorwill who sings: "Whippoorwill, whippoorwill, whippoorwill."

LILA (CONT'D)
Hey there, little bird. I got _my_ song right, too.

Then, with the lantern, journal and suitcase, Lila hurries to the road without looking back.

And the whippoorwill takes flight into the deep blue sky.